Johnny Cash

Johnny Cash

Michael Heatley

CHARTWELL
BOOKS

This edition published in 2014 by
CHARTWELL BOOKS
an imprint of Book Sales
a division of Quarto Publishing Group USA Inc.
276 Fifth Avenue Suite 206
New York, New York 10001
USA

Copyright © 2014 by Greene Media Ltd.,
34 Dean Street, Brighton BN1 3EG

Design by Greene Media Ltd

ISBN-13: 978-0-7858-3151-8

Printed and bound in China

CREDITS

Thanks to all those who helped with the photos used in this book, particularly Claire at Corbis and Philip at Getty Images. All photos are credited below, where possible. If anyone has been miscredited or missed out, please contact the Publisher and the correction will be made at the earliest possibility.

Cover images:
Front: Michael Ochs Archives/Getty Images
CD: Michael Ochs Archives/Getty Images
Back: Bettmann/Corbis

8B, Abernathyautoparts via wikicommons; 9 wikicommons; 11 from "Inside Johnny Cash's Boyhood Home" at LiveFastDiePoor.com; 27 dave–7 via wikicommons.

Corbis: 97T, 121, 125; 1, 26, 30, 36, 38, 62 Marvin Koner; 6 Michael Ochs Archives; 7, 60, 70, 82, 84–89, 95, 97B, 99R, 101, 102, 112R, 128, 132 (both), 133, 134, 135 (both), 165L Bettmann; 8, 174 John Atashian; 12–13, 29 Andrew Lichtenstein; 21 John Van Hasselt; 28 Paul Kitagaki Jr/ZUMA Press; 104B Chris Hoffmann/dpa; 108 Steve Dozier/ZUMA Press; 115 Laura Farr/ZUMA; 120 Karen Kasmauski; 123B Lynn Goldsmith; 131 (both) Christopher Berkey/epa; 143, 146 Christopher Little; 152, 153 (both) Kevin Estrada/Retna Ltd; 155 Vivian Ronay/Retna Ltd; 168, 169 John Sommers/Reuters; 180 Jeff Christensen/Reuters; 183L Katy Winn; 185 USPS/Splash News

Getty Images: 56, 58, 118T, 145, 159, 161–163, 167, 171, 172, 175–177L, 178–179, 183R, 184; 2 Time & Life Pictures; 5 Harry Langdon; 14, 16, 20, 23, 25, 31, 33, 34, 37, 41–51, 61 (all), 62TL, 63, 67, 71 (both), 72, 74, Michael Ochs Archives; 17, 18, 53, 54, 57, 62TR, 69 (inset), 75, 78, 79R, 81, 96, 98T, 104T, 106, 118B, 119, 122, 123T, 127, 137, 138 (both) Redferns; 32, 52, 59R, 76, 79L, 83, 99L, 148, 151, 189 Hulton Archive; 55 David Gahr; 129, 130 ABC; 64, 65, 98B, 100, 112L Moviepix; 69, 77, 141, 142 Time & Life Pictures; 80, 103 CBS; 91 (both), 93 (both), 144, 147, 156, 158, 165R WireImage; 92 *NY Daily News*; 105 Fairfax Media; 107 Popperfoto; 109, 110, 111 (both) JP Laffont/Sygma; 113 Robert Alexander; 114 Pictorial Parade; 116–117 UIG; 126, 157, 181, 182 AFP; 139 Ron Galella Collection/WireImage; 140 Jack Vartoogian; 149 NBCU Photo Bank; 160 Janette Beckman; 164 Rusty Russell; 173 FilmMagic, Inc

PAGE 1: Johnny Cash watches performers from backstage before he goes out to perform in White Plains, New York in 1959.

PAGE 2: Cash regularly sang about railroads and trains. This *Time Life* photoshoot dates to 1969.

RIGHT: Johnny Cash in 2002.

CONTENTS

Introduction	**6**
1 Early Life 1932–1954	**10**
2 Breakthrough with Sun 1955–1957	**24**
3 Columbia Bound 1958–1965	**40**
Johnny's Guitars	**58**
On the Road	**60**
Movie Debut	**64**
4 The Outlaw 1965–1970	**66**
Cash in Britain	**78**
Prison Albums	**82**
Madison Square Garden	**90**
5 The Man in Black 1970–1989	**94**
The Johnny Cash Show	**128**
6 Rejuvenation 1990–1997	**136**
Cash Unchained	**152**
7 Final Years	**154**
8 The Legacy	**166**
Top Tunes: A Select Discography of Hits	**186**
What's on the CD	**188**
Index	**190**

INTRODUCTION

"Suffice it to say that few people have been as powerful and influential as Johnny Cash, and the world is a much poorer place for his absence."
Moby

Johnny Cash, the self-styled "Man In Black," has transcended the country genre to become a popular music icon. He was one of the most influential musicians of the 20th century, writing over a thousand songs and selling over ninety million albums in his near fifty-year career. His distinctive baritone, "scrubbing" guitar style, and mixture of wry humor and pathos in his songs made him unique not only in country but music as a whole.

From the humblest of beginnings, Cash would go on to release nearly a hundred studio albums, selling millions of records worldwide. An early single on Sun, "Cry, Cry, Cry," cracked the *Billboard* Top 20, but it was 1956's "I Walk The Line," a country chart-topper that crossed over to the pop Top 20, that made the world stand up and take notice. The rockabilly-styled song would go on to sell over two million copies and put him on the map. It also titled an Oscar-winning Hollywood movie, starring Joaquin Phoenix as the man himself.

Other songs that left an indelible mark on popular American culture throughout the decades included "A Boy Named Sue" and the Grammy-award winning "Ring Of Fire." He was inducted into the Country Music, Songwriters, Rock and Roll, and Gospel Halls of Fame, a unique quartet of honors. Cash would record and release albums right up

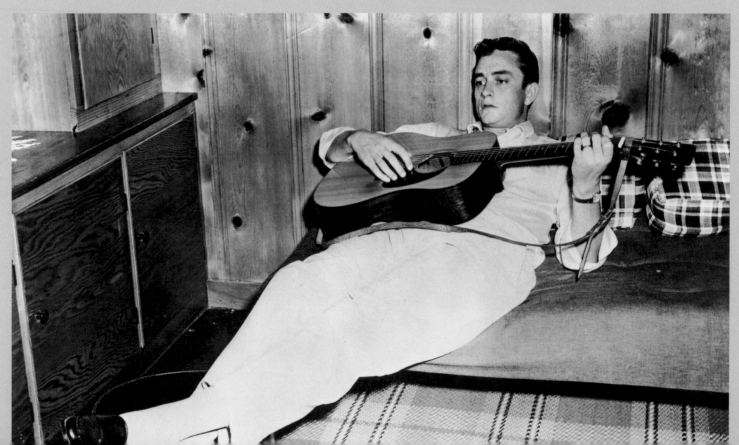

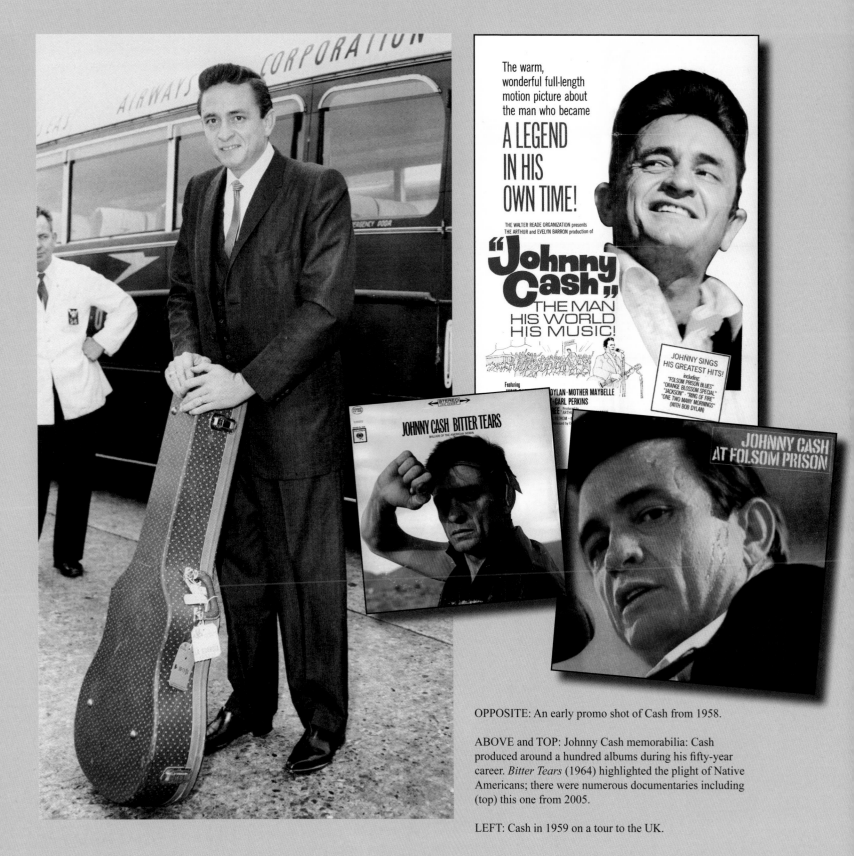

OPPOSITE: An early promo shot of Cash from 1958.

ABOVE and TOP: Johnny Cash memorabilia: Cash produced around a hundred albums during his fifty-year career. *Bitter Tears* (1964) highlighted the plight of Native Americans; there were numerous documentaries including (top) this one from 2005.

LEFT: Cash in 1959 on a tour to the UK.

ABOVE: Playing with The Highwaymen helped extend Cash's career and keep him popular in his later years.

LEFT: Cash in the driver's seat of the "One Piece At a Time" Cadillac that Bruce Fitzpatrick (standing), owner of Abernathy Auto Parts and Hilltop Auto Salvage in Nashville, TN, built to help the song's promotion. The car was presented to Cash in April 1976 by Fitzpatrick and some of the company employees. (See page 110.)

RIGHT: Cash meets President Richard Nixon in the White House, July 1972, as photographed by the president's official photographer, Ollie Atkins.

until his death in 2003 after an illness, during which he still toured and recorded.

Johnny Cash was undoubtedly one of music's most influential artists, yet in 2006 he sat on top of the U.S. album chart for only the second time with *American V: A Hundred Highways*, a success he would sadly not be alive to witness.

His marriage to second wife June Carter in 1968 proved beneficial to both his career and his personal life. Touring and recording together, they would die within months of each other. June proved a stabilizing influence on Cash's addictive personality, saving him from self-destruction on many occasions.

Johnny Cash was not to be the last surviving member of the so-called Million Dollar Quartet—Jerry Lee Lewis having outlived Cash, Elvis Presley, and Carl Perkins—but he turned out a body of music that stands comparison with any 20th-century artist, let alone his Sun labelmates. The fact that, in his later years, he worked with such cutting-edge talents as producer Rick Rubin, songwriter Trent Reznor of Nine Inch Nails, and video director Anton Corbijn, a close collaborator of U2, shows he was never content to rest on past glories.

This book can only scratch the surface of the Johnny Cash story. If it inspires you, seek out the recordings and complete the picture!

EARLY LIFE 1932–1954

"I knew I wanted to sing when I was a very small boy. When I was probably four years old. My mother played a guitar and I would sit with her and she would sing and I learned to sing along with her."

Johnny Cash

Born to Ray Cash, a farmer, and Carrie Rivers Cash, in Kingsland, Arkansas, on February 26, 1932, Johnny Cash began life as plain J.R. Cash. His parents apparently couldn't think of names, so settled on initials. (Other sources claim they couldn't decide between the names John and Ray, so compromised.) When the teenage Cash enlisted in the U.S. Air Force, they wouldn't let him use initials alone, so he started to use the name John R. Cash.

The youngster and his family relocated from his birthplace to Dyess when Cash was three. This was a new community some 250 miles distant but in the same state of Arkansas, named after a local administrator. The two-day journey there was made in a truck, the Cash children, huddled under a tarpaulin for warmth, singing the hymn "I Am Bound For The Promised Land." They would live in a new house, two bedrooms to house the family of eight, but with no electricity or running water.

The Cash family were cotton farmers whose business had been wiped out in the Great Depression. The Government offered a deal whereby failed farmers could buy a house, a barn, and twenty acres of land for no money down, then be given a cow and a mule. They would not be expected to pay back this investment until they harvested their first crop. Cash later called the scheme

"communalism," and its success (forty-six such schemes were set up across the United States) reinforced his idea that humans should work together for the common good rather than subscribe to the standard American capitalist ethos.

The first Cash, William, had sailed his ship, the *Good Intent*, from Glasgow and settled in Massachusetts in 1667. (When Johnny researched his paternal heritage, he concluded that he was of Scottish royal descent, and that his line could be traced back to Malcolm IV of Scotland.) His descendants migrated from Massachusetts to Virginia and Georgia; Johnny's Georgia-born great-grandfather Reuben Cash fought for the Confederacy in the Civil War and survived to tell the tale.

Father Ray had tales of his own to tell, and was a big influence on the young JR. He'd been one of twelve children and had become the breadwinner of his family at just fifteen when Reuben died. Ray's quest for employment to keep his own family going in those Depression days took him far and wide, jumping railroad boxcars to reach the next job that offered cash in hand. His return was always eagerly awaited.

Johnny remembered his father as "a man of love. He always loved me to death. He worked hard in the fields, but my father never hit me. Never. I don't ever remember a

The house in Dyess where Cash and his family lived after 1935 has been rescued from dereliction and become a place of pilgrimage.

A tractor plows a field next to Johnny Cash's boyhood home in rural Dyess, Arkansas. During the Great Depression, Dyess was organized into a farming cooperarive that grew and sold its crops collectively. It was part of a New Deal program to rescue the area from severe poverty.

really cross, unkind word from my father." It was Ray who carried Johnny the last hundred yards to his new home through thick Arkansas mud, the truck being unable to make it any further up the road.

But there was another side to Ray Cash; he had an addictive personality, and would have violent rages after he had been drinking. It was in one such fit of temper that he killed the young JR's dog. Cash admits to having inherited his father's "addictive behavior" and fought hard not to inherit his rage too.

As a boy, Cash was fascinated by the original *Frankenstein* movie. For him, the monster was a sympathetic character, someone "made up of bad parts but trying to do good." It was a duality he saw in his father and would recognize in himself.

Cash spent his childhood and youth on his parents' farm, working the fields with his father and his siblings. His first job, at age four, was as a "water boy," taking drinks out to the adults toiling in the fields, but he would soon graduate to more arduous tasks. One byproduct of working with older people was that he started smoking when he was twelve years old. He also used to eat young cotton buds, despite his mother's warnings that they would give him stomach ache.

Music was his escape route from this demanding world of work. "I picked cotton by hand, from the age of five until I was eighteen years old, every day, after school, right until dark. I would sing to myself when I walked home from the fields at night. Songs were my magic to take me through the dark places." This was confirmed when, in 1944, he saw harmony-based country duo the Louvin Brothers, who came to Dyess in a traveling show. Cash was too shy to ask Charlie and Ira for an autograph, but decided there and then that a singer was what he was going to be.

Work songs chanted by field hands, the sound of freight trains rolling by, the family piano, and the music of the Pentecostal Church of God (Cash accepted Christ at the age of twelve)—all played a part in shaping his musical outlook. His surroundings would inspire songs: the 1937 flood evacuation of Dyess, for instance, is immortalized in the 1959 song "Five Feet High and Rising."

He treasured his closeness with his five brothers and sisters—Roy, Jack, Tommy (later a country singer), Reba, and Joann. But tragedy struck when, in 1943, his beloved older brother Jack died in an horrific accident. "I felt like I'd died too," he later confessed. "It was terribly lonely without him. I had no other friend."

While cutting wood, Jack was sliced through the middle by a power saw. He was slow to die, the family gathering around his hospital bed to sing hymns. On his last day Jack sat up in bed and asked if they could "hear the angels." He said they shouldn't worry, he was going to "a beautiful place."

Cash revealed in his autobiography a premonition that his brother should not go to work that day but join him fishing, but Jack was determined to bring some money home. He wrote, "There was no way around grief and there's no way around loss and nothing is ever the same after it."

In the summer of 1944, he went to Boy Scout camp and talked of nothing but Jack; however, his fellow scouts grew tired of hearing him and told him it was time to give it a rest. "I got the message," Cash said. "I quit talking about Jack altogether. Everybody knew how I felt and how my mother felt; they didn't need us telling them." His feeling of guilt was made no better by father Ray pointing out the irony that the hardworking Jack was killed while the good-for-nothing layabout who chose fishing over work lived on.

His brother's death was one of many events that would inspire songs. Decades later, Cash spoke of looking forward to meeting his brother in heaven, while in 2002, just before his own death, he admitted: "There's never been two months gone by that I haven't dreamed about him. He's tried to help turn me to the [Christian] way of life."

As Cash was growing up he was listening to a wide variety of music—sentimental old-time ballads, traditional country, blues, and gospel—that represented his musical roots and would find expression in his own output. Cash began playing guitar and writing songs when given an instrument at the age of twelve. He was taught his first chords by his mother and a childhood friend called Jesse Barnhill, who had polio, and so chose guitar-playing over physical pursuits.

Favorite radio shows on Cash's dial included *Smilin' Eddie Hill's High Noon Round-Up* from WMPS/Memphis, which featured the first group he'd ever seen, the Louvin Brothers; he caught this every day on his lunch break. The first song he heard on a radio was "Hobo Bill's Last Ride" by Jimmie Rodgers, the legendary Singing Brakeman. Grand Ole Opry broadcasts were the highlights of Friday and Saturday nights, featuring the music of Ernest Tubb, Roy Acuff, and Hank Williams.

Cash admired the pioneering work of Williams—so much so that, following his departure from his first record label, Sun, he left behind enough material for them to issue the album *Johnny Cash Sings Hank Williams*. The same year of 1960 also saw him pay tribute to his influences by recording a batch of tunes made famous by his favorite country singers. The result was the album *Now, There Was A Song!* His links to his musical heritage were affectionate and clear.

OPPOSITE: Country singer Charlie Louvin (left) holds an acousic guitar and his brother Ira holds his mandolin as the Louvin Brothers pose for a portrait on the back of a train. They were early influences on Johnny Cash as he plotted his own musical course.

ABOVE: Pictured in 1944, Huddie Ledbetter, universally known as Leadbelly, wrote songs Cash covered as he tapped into a similar folky vein of music.

OPPOSITE: Concert poster for Maybelle Carter and the Carter Sisters.

Johnny's connections with the legendary Carter Family, who graced the U.S. airwaves between the wars, were strengthened when he married his second wife, June Carter, in 1968. But the family's radio broadcasts, in which June's mother Maybelle was a prime participant, had inspired him when he was growing up. Another early influence was Leadbelly, the folk-blues pioneer born Huddie Ledbetter whose "Goodnight Irene" Cash covered for Sun in 1957. "On A Monday" formed the basis for "I Got Stripes," a highlight of Cash's Folsom Prison performance in 1968—but, since Leadbelly died in 1949, there was never likely to be a copyright problem.

The young Cash homed in on railroad songs like the story of Casey Jones, a ballad from 1928 by bluesman Furry Lewis that told a story that is part of American folklore. In the early 1900s, Jones was driving the Cannonball Express between Memphis, Tennessee, and Canton, Mississippi when he roared around a blind bend in the track and crashed into the rear of another train. When his body was found, one hand was on the air brake and the other on the whistle, having told his fireman to jump for his life.

"The Wreck Of The Old 97" was another classic American railroad ballad from the early 20th century that found its way into the Cash repertoire. The story of the derailment of Southern Railway fast mail train No. 97 near Danville, Virginia, is said to have been the American music industry's first million-seller for Vernon Dalhart in 1924.

When he began singing in earnest, Cash had a high tenor voice which had yet to develop into the familiar bass tones we associate with him. "Suddenly my voice dropped and I was singing bomm—buh-buh—bomm, way down low in the key of E. And my mother said, 'Who is that singing?' She came out of the back door and there I was…"

He took only three singing lessons, at the bidding of his mother who took in washing to make the $3 each of them cost. After the third, his teacher—"a young, kind, and very pretty" woman, as he later recalled—advised him not to let anyone change the way he sang. He was pleased, but regretted in later life not learning how to look after his voice rather than abusing it. It was a God-given gift of which he was "the bearer, not the owner."

After graduating from Dyess High School in 1950, teenager Cash spent a brief period in Michigan working at the Fisher auto body plant in Pontiac, a stint that lasted less than a month. Returning home, he found the family farm so run down that his father had found work in a margarine factory. He followed suit, but conditions were appalling and, as he sought more amenable employment, "a government pay check and a clean blue uniform looked pretty good." He followed the path of many Southern male teens and enlisted in the U.S. Air Force, just a week before the Korean War broke out. He found himself based in Germany, working as a radio operator. The four-year tour of duty, he later said, "taught me how to cuss, how to look for women, how to drink and fight."

His job with the U.S. Air Force Security Service required him to use his ears and intercept Soviet radio communications. He was the first man outside Russia to learn of Stalin's death, while he tracked the first Soviet jet-powered bomber's maiden flight from Moscow to Smolensk. There were two listening stations, the other in the Aleutian Islands off Alaska. Cash, whose unique skills stopped him from being posted to Korea, enjoyed being in Germany, where, thanks to the time difference, he could use his radio equipment to tune into the Grand Ole Opry on Sunday mornings as it was being transmitted in the States on a Saturday night.

Cash bought his first decent guitar for twenty German marks, the equivalent of $5, walking back four miles to his camp through the snow as he had no money remaining. He used the time between shifts to learn to play and, with his savings from his $85 monthly pay, bought a reel-to-reel tape machine. This helped him write songs that would later

DAVID CROCKETT THEATRE
LAWRENCEBURG - TENN.
WED MATINEE & NITE SEP 10

CARTER SISTERS
FEATURING
MOTHER MAYBELLE
DIRECT FROM
WSM GRAND OLE OPRY

Johnny Cash and Luther Perkins in 1950.

become famous—such as "I Walk The Line." Legend has it he accidentally spooled a tape of his four-piece group, the Landberg Barbarians, to play backwards; the droning sound that resulted inspired his writing style.

Among the titles he penned around that time were "Balshazar," a gospel song he later described as "the first song I wrote that I intended to record," and "Folsom Prison Blues." The latter, vastly different in content if not style, was inspired by a movie he saw at the base, *Inside The Walls Of Folsom Prison*, and contained probably his most famous ever line, "I shot a man in Reno just to watch him die."

Unlike Elvis Presley later in the decade, who spent most of his time secluded in his army base, Cash's spell in the military inspired him to appreciate the customs of other countries. He visited Spain and Britain, where he was among the crowds at the coronation of Queen Elizabeth II in 1953. He was discharged with the rank of sergeant in 1954, after declining the offer of a permanent commission.

Johnny had a good reason to return to the States in the shape of Vivian Liberto. They had met at a roller-skating rink in her hometown of San Antonio in July 1951, shortly before he was shipped out to Europe. She was still a schoolgirl two years his junior. He'd finally plucked up courage to ask her for a skate near closing time—and though he wasn't very steady on his feet, he impressed her by singing along to a Rosemary Clooney tune playing over the loudspeakers at the time.

The couple announced their engagement after a whirlwind three-week romance. The love letters they wrote each other while they were apart amounted to some 10,000 pages—Cash wrote all his in green ink—while he left behind the romantic message "Johnny Loves Vivian" carved in a bench on San Antonio's River Walk.

Vivian Liberto and Johnny Cash married in her home town on August 7, 1954, a little more than a month after the groom's return from his tour of duty in Europe. The ceremony at St. Ann's Catholic church was performed by Vivian's uncle, Father Vincent Liberto. Cash then headed to Memphis, Tennessee, with his new wife.

At that stage his musical ambitions were relatively modest. "The extent of my dream was to sing on the radio station in Memphis. That was the big thing when I was growing up, singing on the radio. Even when I got out of the Air Force in 1954, I came right back to Memphis and started knocking on doors at the radio station."

While waiting for his break Cash was earning his livelihood as an electrical appliance salesman, selling door to door, but grew to hate it. The boss of the company, George Bates, recognized that he was no salesman but employed him anyway and, over time, advanced him over a thousand dollars to help him get his music career off the ground. Cash, who described Bates as "one of those angels," was happy to write him out a cheque for the full sum when he made it.

His luck had changed for the better when brother Roy introduced him to two friends. Marshall Grant and Luther Perkins shared Cash's love for "hillbilly" music; both were four or five years older, and had formerly played in the Dixie Rhythm Ramblers. A fourth man—A.W. "Red" Kernodle, ten years their senior—was also involved at the very start.

All four guitar players jammed together, and the results were unspectacular. Then Grant perceptively said to Perkins and Cash, "Somebody's gotta learn how to play lead guitar and somebody's gotta learn how to play bass if we expect to have any success like Elvis has had." So Luther said, "I know where I can get an electric guitar," and came back with a borrowed Fender Telecaster with its volume control stuck at maximum.

This problem led Perkins to develop the practice of muting the three bass strings (E, A, and D) with the heel of his right hand, in the style of Merle Travis, and scratching a rhythm pattern. This would become an integral part of his and Cash's sound. Kernodle moved to steel guitar, but this

required greater skill and he would duck out of their Sun audition, not wanting to hold them back. (As it happened, Sam Phillips disliked steel guitar, so this was an advantage.)

Perkins told Grant there was a used Kay upright bass for sale, which he promptly bought. Grant gave Cash his acoustic guitar, the best one they owned between them, and they began to teach themselves how to play. Not only did they teach themselves, but Perkins and Grant, soon to be known as the Tennessee Two, created a sound that has not only stood the test of time but has also been an inspiration to countless musicians around the world.

"The Johnny Cash sound was created by the three of them equally, you know what I mean?" Rosanne Cash, Johnny's eldest daughter and a musician herself, later said. "There was none of that 'boom chicka boom' without Marshall. You can't separate the three of them at that point when it all started. It was one thing."

Grant wasn't trained on the bass, and had to fix tape to the instrument's neck to tell him where the notes were. It took all three of them to figure out how to tune the instrument, but Grant's contributions to the sound eventually proved as essential as they were rudimentary. None of the trio was a skilled musician, but against the odds their combined limitations helped create a sound that was instantly identifiable.

"So many people think we took ten years creating this style," Grant later explained. "It was there in the first eight bars (of music) we played, and we spent the next four years trying to get rid of it."

Johnny Cash was now up front and at the center of the stage show, a position he would never relinquish. His first gig with the Tennessee Two backing him was playing for a group of elderly ladies in a church basement—the trio of Cash, Perkins, and Grant all dressed in dark clothes as Johnny—who in those struggling days "didn't own a suit, or even a tie"—decided dressing alike would make them look more like a real band. All went well, so they continued with

OPPOSITE: Johnny Cash performs with the Tennessee Three (drummer W.S. Holland, bassist Marshall Grant, and guitarist Luther Perkins) at the New York Folk Festival in July 1965.

BELOW: The Sun Studios in Memphis, where Johnny Cash followed in the pioneering footsteps of Elvis Presley. Like Elvis, however, he would find greater financial rewards elsewhere.

SUN RECORDS

"You build on failure. You use it as a stepping stone. Close the door on the past. You don't try to forget the mistakes, but you don't dwell on it. You don't let it have any of your energy, or any of your time, or any of your space."

Johnny Cash

the sartorial theme for a while before the other two reverted to lighter clothing. Cash's beloved mother Carrie hated him wearing dark clothes and, for a while, he relented. But the "bright, flashy" outfits made for him by wife Vivian—including a white suit with glittering blue trim—didn't sit easily with the music and he reverted to wearing black "because I liked it." In 1971, it would inspire one of his most famous songs, and even in later years he maintained his fashion code "as a symbol of my rebellion."

Another advantage, of course, was that black was easier to keep clean on long tours. Fellow acts teased him about it, calling him the Undertaker, but the Man in Black's career was far from dead and buried. He would have the last laugh as his talents proved far brighter than his chosen apparel.

Perkins and Grant were at Cash's side when he approached Sun Records' Sam Phillips in March 1955 asking for a chance to record and become a labelmate of Elvis Presley, Roy Orbison, Carl Perkins, and Jerry Lee Lewis. The songs they played at the audition that day have been a subject of much debate: some say they performed Cash originals "Wide Open Road" and "You're My Baby," but others have disputed this.

Whatever was played, that visit to his local studio would change his life forever. "Baby, we're cuttin' a record!" was his greeting to Vivian, heavily pregnant with their first child, when he came home.

OPPOSITE: Cash poses for an early publicity handout in 1955 in Memphis, TN. It identified his agents as Stars Inc.

BREAKTHROUGH WITH SUN 1955–1957

"Johnny Cash could have gone by the wayside if I had tried to make a rocker out of him. Johnny Cash had folk all over him."
Sam Phillips

The Sun Studios at 706 Union Avenue, Memphis, Tennessee, was, quite simply, the birthplace of rock'n'roll. When Elvis Presley first passed through the doors one Saturday in the summer of 1953 he began a cultural revolution.

Johnny Cash would follow Presley into the studio two years later and begin a career that would also become legendary. Like Elvis, his popularity would span the decades and transcend age, nationality, and gender.

A former radio announcer, Sam Phillips had launched the Memphis Recording Service (MRS) on the Union Avenue site a few years earlier, recording any occasion and selling the results to the participants. He remembered: "I had to do everything I possibly could do to get those doors open—I wasn't going to turn anything down. I just about did anything as long as it was half-way legal!"

After an ill-fated attempt at forming a record label, Phillips began recording artists through MRS, leasing the recordings to larger labels. Sun was created in February 1952, and by the time Cash arrived in the spring of 1955 Phillips had upgraded his primitive equipment. He installed two Ampex 350 reel-to-reel recorders, the second providing the essential tape-delay echo or slapback that gave the Sun sound such a vibrant, three-dimensional quality.

Elvis had released just five singles on Sun before manager Colonel Tom Parker moved him on to RCA in late 1955 for $40,000—a large amount of money for a struggling concern such as Sam's. The "transfer fee" ensured the cash-strapped Sun's survival although it lost the company its biggest star and a bigger fortune. Carl Perkins was the next man in line, but it would be Cash who proved the nearest thing to Elvis' successor.

The first time Cash spoke to Phillips on the telephone, he'd introduced himself as a gospel singer, only to be immediately rebuffed. "Sam said, 'We can't sell gospel records'," he later recalled. "So a couple of weeks later I called him back again and said, 'I'm John Cash'—he didn't remember that I'd called before—and I told him I'd like to come down and sing him some songs."

Johnny has more than one version of how he finally got through the front door at Sun: "When I got out of the Air Force I went and knocked on that door and was turned away. So one morning I found out what time [Sam Phillips] went to work. I went down with my guitar and sat on his steps until he got there. I introduced myself and he said, 'You're the one that's been calling.'

I said, 'Yeah.' I had to take the chance. Evidently, he woke up on the right side of the bed that morning."

Cash tunes his guitar before a stage performance.

Sun Records boss Sam Phillips takes a piano lesson from Jerry Lee Lewis.

When Cash auditioned at Sun, he hoped to record the gospel music he grew up on. Phillips had an eye for talent but, as he didn't believe gospel would sell. he persuaded Cash to perform in the style that was bringing the label success with artists such as Elvis and Carl Perkins—rock'n'roll.

Phillips later explained why he steered Cash away from songs of faith and towards "the Devil's music."

"While I loved selling gospel as much as anybody, it just wasn't the right time for us. Johnny apologized to me about not having a steel and fiddle when he auditioned. And yet I said, 'Man, I absolutely feel the overall thing here, and it's in a category by itself.' "

When this rock'n'roll summit meeting was recreated in the 2005 movie *Walk The Line*, Joaquin Phoenix, who plays Cash, holds his acoustic guitar across his chest like a boy with a grownup instrument too big for him: a distinctive gesture. When he and his companions audition for Phillips with a dull gospel number, Phillips curtly silences Cash, and challenges him to imagine being hit by an automobile and sing the song he'd want to be remembered for. If true, it's tempting to suggest that

this is where Cash's dark, melancholy, passionate style was born.

Whatever the truth, the result of that meeting of minds in Memphis was the single "Hey Porter." Backed with "Cry, Cry, Cry" (recorded in May 1955) as Sun 221, it would edge out Elvis Presley and Johnny's early heroes the Louvin Brothers to make the local #1 spot that summer and hit #14 on *Billboard*'s country chart. When he received his first royalty check, for $2.41, the die was cast, and Johnny Cash the recording artist was born. Daughter Rosanne duly appeared on May 24, 1955, the first of four daughters he and Vivian would have over the next seven years.

Received wisdom has it that Vivian stayed at home and let Johnny get on with his career. It seems, however, that she accompanied her husband on tour in the beginning of his career, leaving their first two daughters Rosanne and Kathy with Vivian's parents. Only with the birth of child number three, Cindy, did she stay home.

Like most young American males Cash was car-mad, and after putting a down payment on a house his next purchase was a 1954 Plymouth Savoy. He would later deem this his

LEFT: A 1954 Plymouth Savoy similar to the one Cash drove in the mid-1950s.

LEFT: Aerial view of Folsom State Prison, CA, immortalized in song by Johnny Cash in 1955.

OPPOSITE: Prisoners on the famous tiered housing units of Old Folsom Prison in California. It was after seeing a film about conditions inside the prison that Cash wrote his famous "Folsom Prison Blues."

dream mobile, all gleaming chrome and whitewall tires, "The best car I ever owned," leading to an early-1970s ad campaign fronted by the singer. This also inspired a contest to find the country's nicest 1954 Plymouth Savoy.

That heady summer of 1955 saw Johnny Cash and his two supporting musicians wedge themselves and his double bass (or "bull fiddle") into his shiny new Plymouth and head out on the road. Cash & the Tennessee Two appeared at local Memphis venues with Elvis Presley (who paid him $75 a show) and landed a regular spot on the KWEM Saturday radio program.

The most memorable show of the year came late in the year at Shreveport at the Louisiana Hayride. While not as prestigious as the Grand Ole Opry, the Saturday-night show was broadcast far and wide on the radio waves and had proved a significant stepping-stone for the likes of Faron Young, Webb Pierce and Hank Williams on their way to the Opry and national fame.

Shreveport was the first place Cash heard himself on the radio and he got a thrill out of hearing the audience sing along to his hits. But the highs and the lows, the temptations, and eventually, the strains of leaving his young family behind would cause stress he alleviated with pills.

He took his first amphetamine in 1957 while on tour with Ferlin Husky and Faron Young and enjoyed the feeling of energy it gave him. He likened it to "electricity turning on a light bulb," and was happy it reduced his shyness off stage and helped him mix more easily with people.

He was able to obtain these pills by prescription, telling the doctors he was working late hours and driving long distances so needed to keep awake. But the amount needed to have any effect kept going up as his tolerance grew and the "crashes" between doses more extreme. The damage it ultimately did to his own mental and physical health, his relationships with others and his marriage to Vivian were regrets he took with him to his grave, despite repeated attempts to make amends.

In December 1955, the Cash-penned "Folsom Prison Blues" (a song originally pitched to Tennessee Ernie Ford of "Sixteen Tons" fame) was released, making #4 on the country chart. It earned him a second royalty check, this time for $6,000. The song was significant, as Cash's alignment with the disadvantaged and those behind bars began with "Folsom Prison Blues."

"The prisoners heard that song and they felt like I was one of them. They'd treat me like I was one of them." His words sounded authentic, even though the singer never spent more than a night in a police cell (seven times in total) on misdemeanor charges, and led to an association with prisons that lasted many years.

The success of this recording led to him being invited to appear at the Huntsville, Texas, prison rodeo in 1956. He, Luther, and Marshall had defied a torrential rainstorm that had caused Perkins' guitar amplifier to short-circuit and Grant's bass to fall apart; they played on regardless, and it was the beginning of a legend.

The first day of the following year saw the Tennessee Two play at San Quentin Prison's annual New Year's show. The gig went so well that it became an annual booking and would eventually lead to a best-selling live LP, recorded there in 1969. This—the only #1 album Cash would register

OPPOSITE: Cash in 1959.

ABOVE: Cash and Vivian Liberto, his first wife and mother to his four daughters.

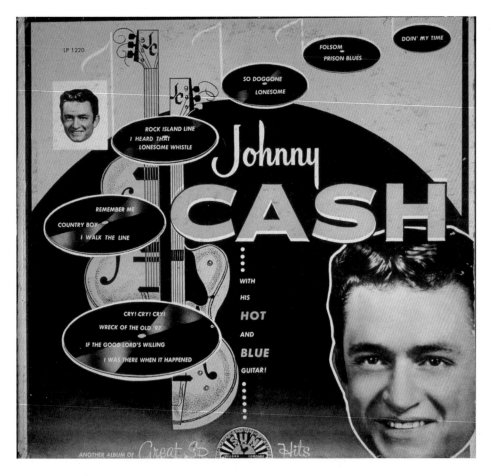

time, but Perkins saw potential in it and suggested a change of title from "Because You're Mine" to something more original. Cash, inspired once more, finished the song, now re-christened "I Walk The Line," in less than the time it took Perkins to complete his set. (In return, it's said, Cash gave his friend the idea for the rock'n'roll classic "Blue Suede Shoes," based on the flashy wardrobe of an Air Force colleague stationed in Germany.)

"I Walk The Line," released by Sun back in 1956, remains Johnny Cash's best-known single release. He scored his first major hit with the song and it was the source of the title of the 2005 biopic *Walk the Line* as well as a non-biographical 1970 movie starring Gregory Peck which used his songs as the soundtrack. The idea of walking a line between good and bad was also a metaphor for the religious yet paradoxical Cash's life.

Cash was the first Sun artist to make an album, and he released two LPs while at Sun, *Johnny Cash With His Hot And Blue Guitar* and *Sings The Songs That Made Him Famous*. After he left for the larger CBS/Columbia label, *Greatest!* was released by Sun Records in January 1959 to coincide with Cash's debut album for his new label. Their decision to "cash in" on the singer's popularity was a treat for fans regardless of its motive, as the album contained classic tracks and showcased previously unheard work he did with the Memphis recording company.

The B-sides and unreleased tracks included covers such as Hank Williams' "Hey Good Lookin'" and "You Win Again," as well as Cash-penned numbers like "Luther Played The Boogie" and the smash hit "Get Rhythm" that reached #1 in the country charts. It was well received by Cash fans, who considered it a fine selection of tracks from his early career.

Interestingly, "Get Rhythm" had been the result of an invitation by Elvis to write a song especially for him (he also wrote a song for Roy Orbison, "You're My Baby"). But when Elvis switched from Sun to RCA, Sam Phillips had

in his lifetime—would be the cherry on the cake of a successful decade.

For now, though, Johnny Cash was constructing the foundations of his mighty career. And when "I Walk The Line," released in the fall of 1956, hit #1 on the country charts and even crossed over to pop, charting at #17 late in the year—Sam Phillips had found another diamond.

The song had sprung from the difficulties Cash found staying faithful to his new wife Vivian, stuck alone back home with their child. Women were now freely available to the once-shy young man, and he was "having a hard time resisting the temptation to be unfaithful…I put those feelings into the beginnings of a song."

He played the result to Carl Perkins while the pair were backstage at a show. It only amounted to two verses at that

Cash and Sam Phillips celebrate sales of "I Walk the Line," the singer's Sun single that put him on the music map.

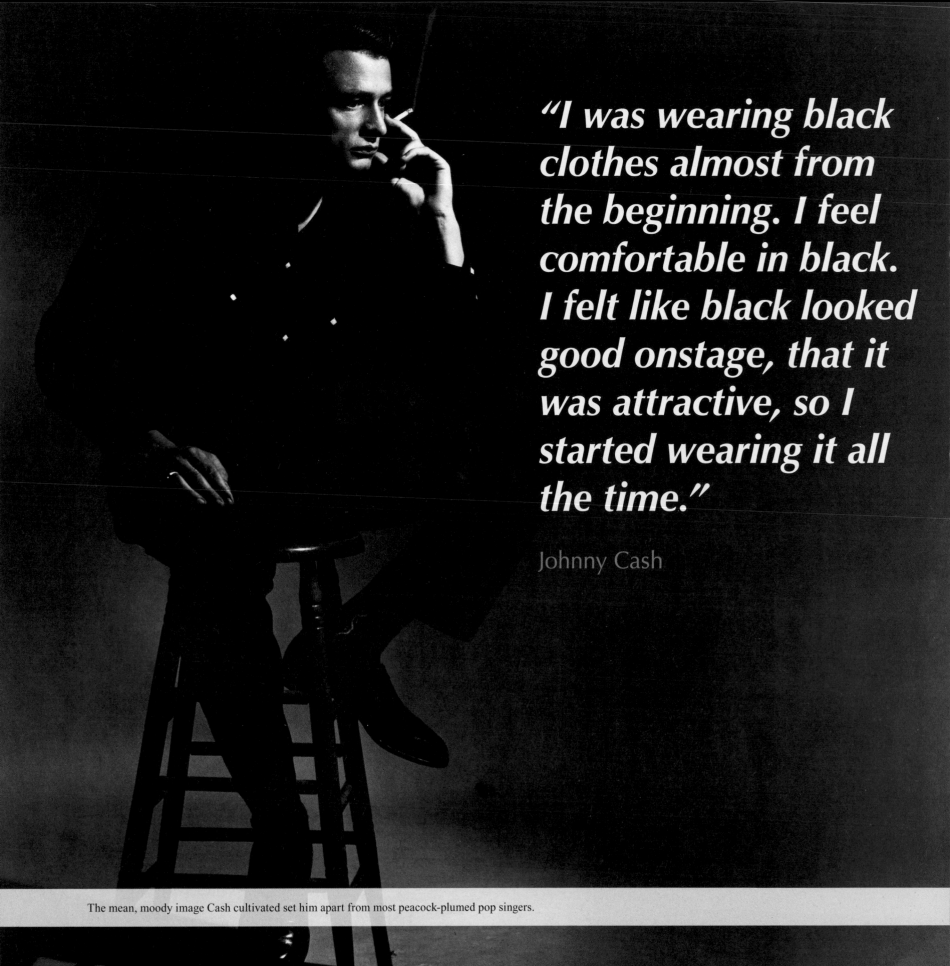

"I was wearing black clothes almost from the beginning. I feel comfortable in black. I felt like black looked good onstage, that it was attractive, so I started wearing it all the time."

Johnny Cash

The mean, moody image Cash cultivated set him apart from most peacock-plumed pop singers.

insisted Cash record it himself rather than let another label benefit.

There had been a one-off reunion involving Cash, Presley, Carl Perkins, and Jerry Lee Lewis in December 1956 which went down in history as the Million Dollar Quartet sessions. Perkins had been recording in the studio that afternoon, attempting to re-establish momentum after promotion of his single "Blue Suede Shoes" had been halted by a serious car crash. Pianist Lewis was assisting at the request of Sam Phillips, who wanted to add a new dimension to Perkins' sound. Being a young artist, Lewis was strapped for cash and was happy to lend a hand.

As the session drew to a close, Elvis arrived to see his old friend Carl, whom he had grown close to after they had played the bars of the mid-South while trying to establish themselves. And while Johnny Cash was the fourth man in the studio, debate has raged as to whether he was present for the whole session. Rumor had it that Phillips recognized the importance of what he was witnessing and, sensing a photo opportunity, summoned him some way into proceedings. However, Cash himself denied this and claimed he was present from the off, explaining that he was singing in a different key in order to keep up with Presley.

The four performers started singing an array of gospel songs, in deference to their roots, before playing several rockier numbers. Most of these were covers of previously released tracks that had influenced them, though they also showcased their own songs. Sam Phillips knew he had something and called Bob Johnson, entertainment editor for local newspaper the *Memphis Press Scimitar*, who brought a photographer to capture the moment. The next day Johnson coined the "Million Dollar Quartet" phrase in his headline. The result has been much reissued over the years.

Cash's run of singles continued with "There You Go" (a country #1), "Next In Line" and "Home Of The Blues." The year of 1958 saw him team with new producer Jack

With His Hot And Blue Guitar

Released: October 1957

Recorded: September 1954 – August 1957

Label: Sun

Producer: Sam Phillips

The first LP ever issued on the Sun Records label.

Side One

1 "Rock Island Line" (Leadbelly) – 2:11

2 "(I Heard That) Lonesome Whistle" (Jimmie Davis, Hank Williams) – 2:25

3 "Country Boy" (Johnny Cash) – 1:49

4 "If the Good Lord's Willing" (Jerry Reed) – 1:44

5 "Cry! Cry! Cry!" (Johnny Cash) – 2:29

6 "Remember Me (I'm the One Who Loves You)" (Stuart Hamblen) – 2:01

Side Two

1 "So Doggone Lonesome" (Johnny Cash) – 2:39

2 "I Was There When It Happened" (Jimmie Davis, Fern Jones) – 2:17

3 "I Walk the Line" (Johnny Cash) – 2:46

4 "Wreck of the Old 97" (Norman Blake, Johnny Cash, Bob Johnson) – 1:48

5 "Folsom Prison Blues" (Johnny Cash) – 2:51

6 "Doin' My Time" (Jimmie Skinner) – 2:40

Personnel:

Johnny Cash

Luther Perkins: Guitar

Marshall Grant: Bass

Clement and score country chart-toppers with "Ballad Of A Teenage Queen" (a country #1 for ten weeks) and "Guess Things Happen That Way." Both releases caught the attention of the youth rock'n'roll audience and crossed over to make #14 and #11 in the pop chart.

Sam Phillips' musical vision often clashed with that of Cash, but the singer came to realize that Sam often saw something he himself had yet to recognize. So it was that "Big River," a song written in the back of a car and performed several times as a standard twelve-bar blues, was transformed by a beat and Jack Clement's powerful chording on an open-tuned Gibson semi-acoustic guitar.

His final Sun single while under contract was written by Charlie Rich, another artist who would later find fame away from Sun. "The Ways Of A Woman In Love" backed with "You're The Nearest Thing To Heaven" became his fourth pop Top 40 entry in the fall of 1958, making #24.

Success was all very well, but Johnny Cash was a devoutly religious man and Sam Phillips' unwillingness to allow him to record religious material for Sun played a major part in his decision to leave the label. Cash reflected on the quandary in his autobiography years later: "To record sacred music by a new country singer like me—and some of it original music, songs I'd written myself, that nobody heard—was something (Phillips) just couldn't do. That didn't sit well with me…"

There were also financial factors at work—and Cash, as a husband, father, and breadwinner, could hardly avoid taking these into account. He was unhappy that he was only getting a three-percent royalty while other, larger companies were paying their artists rates of up to five percent. As Sun's biggest-selling artist of the post-Presley era, the difference in his pay packet could have been considerable. In his second autobiography Cash admitted his feeling for Phillips were "mixed; I think he was another of those angels that appear in your life but I'm not sure he treated me properly in a financial sense (I'm not sure he didn't either)."

OPPOSITE: A contemplative Cash pictured before a concert in White Plains, New York.

BELOW: Elvis takes the piano to serenade Marilyn Evans, a showgirl he met in Las Vegas. The rest of the Million Dollar Quartet—from left Jerry Lee Lewis, Carl Perkins, and Johnny Cash—look on.

Cash fundamentally could not understand how his songs, "his babies," could belong to someone else. He admits he "feels bad about not being fluent in music and money" and, in his second autobiography, concluded that any differences he had with Phillips "had been long resolved. I bear no grudge… If there hadn't been for Sam Phillips, I might still be working in a cotton field."

So it was that Johnny Cash decided to emulate labelmate Elvis Presley and leave Sun, ending up at Columbia Records. The father figure who clinched his signing was producer Don Law, who would become Cash's right-hand man on many of his sessions during the next nine years before retiring aged 65.

It was Law who convinced Cash, via a visit to his parents' house in 1958, to sign for the label, and even got Carl

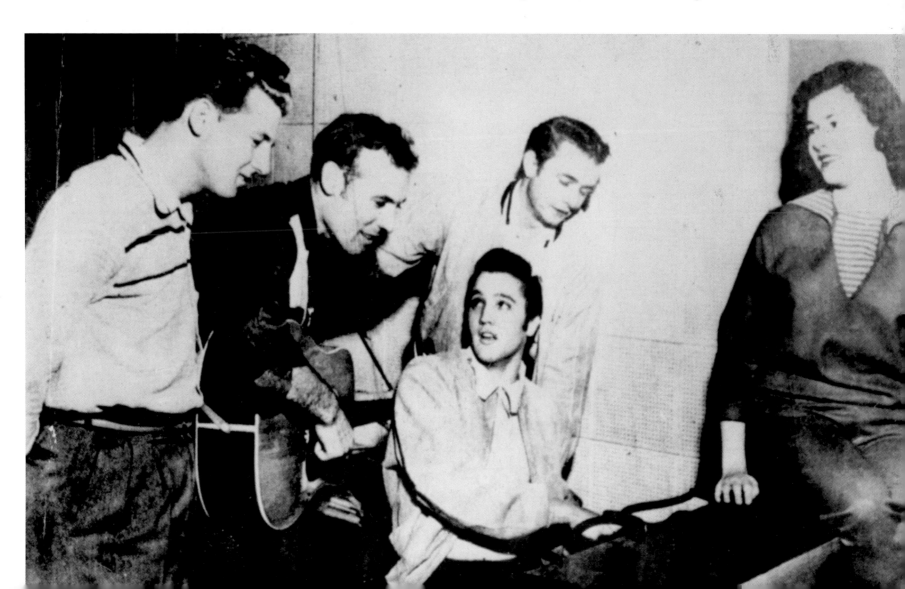

Perkins to join at the same time, at Cash's insistence. Law considered it his biggest coup while at Columbia, though he is also credited as discovering talent like Al Dexter and Southern gospel family quartet the Chuck Wagon Gang.

In 1964, when signing a new contract with Columbia, Johnny Cash paid fulsome tribute to his ally. "If commendations are still a special thing then… I, for whatever it's worth, commend Mr Don Law on his humanity and perseverence."

"I'm sure you fully realise that a country and western A&R [artiste and repertoire] man must be human, down-to-earth, like one of the folks next door because non-business, down-to-earth artists, such as myself, work with them."

"My only regret," he concluded, "is that I wasn't with Columbia Records, and Don Law, from the very first." The suggestion that he should re-record old Sun tracks for the label did not find favor with Cash, who instead insisted on releasing new material. He was determined to make an early mark—and, though he didn't undergo

a dramatic shift in style, the Columbia recordings displayed a much more polished sound and include some Cash classics.

Producers Al Quaglieri and Don Law helped him record his Columbia debut, *The Fabulous Johnny Cash*, released in 1959. But he still had an eye on the gospel market and sessions at Bradley Film & Recording Studio in Nashville, Tennessee between July 1958 and January 1959 yielded *Hymns By Johnny Cash*. His band of Luther Perkins and Marshall Grant was augmented by Buddy Harman on drums and Marvin Hughes on piano.

Careful not to alienate his growing fanbase, Cash mixed gospel overtones with a jaunty country style to produce tracks that are as accessible as the work that had rocketed him to success. Gospel backing singers can be heard on tracks like "I Saw A Man," but opener "It Was Jesus" is classic Cash, albeit with religious content

BELOW: Cash and the Tennessee Two on stage in an early concert prior to recruiting a drummer and adopting the Man in Black image.

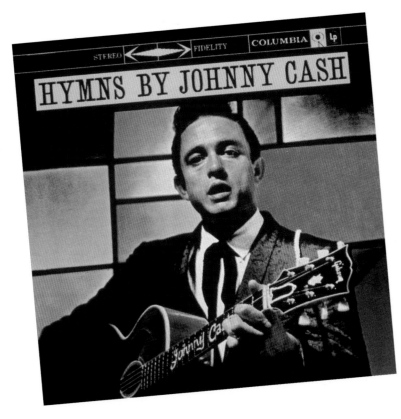

"I am not a Christian artist, I am an artist who is a Christian."
Johnny Cash

Described by Cash as "the album I came to Columbia to record," it did not fare well on its release in May 1959. It failed to chart, perhaps due to its non-commercial nature (there were no hit singles), but received critical acclaim for Cash's sincerity in conveying emotion through the songs, a trait that would continue throughout his career.

Hymns By Johnny Cash is a glimpse at Cash doing what he was born to do, and singing what he believed he was born to sing, though he was keen to make a distinction: "I am not a Christian artist," he said. "I am an artist who is a Christian."

His next studio album would be a return to regular subject-matter; *Songs Of Our Soil*, released a matter of months later, made more of an impact in the musical mainstream. He latched onto the folk revival of the time, with artists such as Harry Belafonte proving the genre's popularity by selling over one million albums.

Producer Law's influence that helped Cash appeal to the folk revival of the time also helped launch the careers of such giants as Bob Dylan and Joan Baez. Under Law's direction, the songs lacked the strings and choirs so often heard on country music of the period, being stripped back to their rhythmic basics.

Songs Of Our Soil, released in September 1959, proved the wisdom of his decision by selling over a million copies. It contained mainly folk ballads, but it was not, strictly speaking, a concept album. It dealt mostly with different facets of American life, but there was a theme of mortality in many of the tracks, something Cash later put down to his growing reliance on drugs, particularly barbiturates.

Growing up on a farm that was once flooded provided the inspiration for the previously mentioned "Five Feet High And Rising." It was released as a single, reaching #14 in the country charts and #76 in the *Billboard* Hot 100. Cash would perform this regularly through his career and, in 1979, members of his family and Arkansas hometown community were filmed and interviewed outside his old homestead to accompany his performance of the song on a TV Christmas Special.

Johnny Cash had begun the 1950s as a single teenager, enroled in the U.S. Air Force and working thousands of miles from home. He ended it as a husband and father and an established recording artist whose career was on the up…yet he was still spending precious little time at home. It was a very long way from the cotton fields of his youth, but underneath he was fundamentally the same person, despite his use of drugs. The decade to come would throw up many more challenges.

3

COLUMBIA BOUND 1958–1965

"I think it speaks to our basic fundamental feelings, you know. Of emotions, of love, of breakup, of love and hate and death and dying, mama, apple pie, and the whole thing. It covers a lot of territory, country music does."

Johnny Cash on *Larry King Live*

Johnny Cash had officially signed for Columbia in 1958. Never one to waste time, he had entered the studio a few weeks before putting pen to paper, in July 1958, to commence recording his first album for the label, *The Fabulous Johnny Cash*. He was joined there by the familiar presence of Luther Perkins and Marshall Grant.

The Tennessee Two's unmistakable, chugging "freight train" style had already become known as the "Johnny Cash sound." "Our inability had more to do with our success than our ability did, and I'm not ashamed of it," Grant once said in an interview.

"Luther played the way he did because he couldn't really play any way else," John Rumble, senior historian at the Country Music Hall of Fame said. "That very sparse, ploughing rhythmic sound was something they just fell into. They didn't just sit there and work on it for weeks. That's pretty much the way they started out."

"It was a highly influential sound," Rumble said. "You had the standard 2/4 beat, the Ray Price shuffle and the Johnny Cash beat—and between those three that covers a whole lot of ground in country music."

Cash himself paid tribute to Luther in his second biography, "He wasn't anything like an expert musician, and sometimes it would take him quite sometime to learn a new song, but once he had it, it was locked in; he'd never alter his part." He also remarked that when they played a 1960s show at a U.S. military base in the United Kingdom, audience member Keith Richards of the Rolling Stones had eyes only for the guitar-player, not the singer.

The Fabulous Johnny Cash had reached #19 on the *Billboard* 200 on its release in January 1959. By this time Cash was a father of two girls, second daughter Kathy (Kathleen) having been born in April 1956. He also had a new manager, Stu Carnall, who convinced him to move to California. In the summer of 1958, the Cash family moved west, initially renting a house in Coldwater Canyon. They then bought a house in Encino previously owned by TV host Johnny Carson at a then amazing cost of $165,000—as much a symbol of his success as a family home.

"At this point," his wife Vivian wrote in a posthumously published autobiography entitled *I Walked The Line: My Life With Johnny*, "I simply agreed with whatever Johnny wanted to do. I can't say I had much of a mind of my own." According to Vivian, this period of time is when Johnny's drinking escalated and he began to have problems with his intake of pills. "All of the things that Johnny had called filthy and dirty [his words from their love letters] and had

Cash and Luther Perkins, the latter playing his famous Telecaster with a stuck volume control, in performance.

ABOVE: Daddy's home. Cash serenades daughters Rosanne and Kathy as first wife Vivian looks on, 1957.

insisted would destroy our lives were things he began to embrace."

A third daughter, Cynthia (known as Cindy), was born in July 1959. An actress and singer who performed with her father in later life, she now believes that, "Pills led Dad into a very destructive period in his life, and Mom paid the price." Her mother was now at home full time and powerless to affect his on-the-road behavior.

Two weeks after their fourth and last daughter, Tara, was born in late summer 1961, the Cashes moved to a hillside home above Nye Road in Casitas Springs, a small community in California's Ojai Valley about fifteen miles from Ventura. Cash bought his parents a trailer park to run to keep them nearby. (Ray would live until 1985, Carrie until 1991.)

A major reason behind the family move was that daughter Rosanne had been found to be allergic to the

Carrie Cash, pictured with her son in the late 1950s, was and would remain a major figure in Johnny's life until her death in 1991.

This set of 1959 photographs taken in Kingsland, Arkansas, teams Cash with good friend Johnny Horton, the singer best known for "The Battle Of New Orleans." Horton, who died the following year in an auto wreck, is pictured preparing fishing lures (right). In 1964, Cash and the Tennessee Three overdubbed backing onto Horton demos of "Rock Island Line" and Hank Williams' "I Just Don't Like This Kind Of Livin'."

Ride This Train

A Stirring Travelogue of America in Song and Story

Released: September 1960
Recorded: December 14–February 16, 1960
Label: Columbia
Producer: Don Law, Al Quaglieri

Side 1
1 "Loading Coal" (Merle Travis) – 4:58
2 "Slow Rider" (Johnny Cash) – 4:12
3 "Lumberjack" (Leon Payne) – 3:02
4 "Dorraine of Ponchartrain" (Johnny Cash) – 4:47

Side 2
1 "Going to Memphis" (Cash, Hollie Dew, Alan Lomax) – 4:26
2 "When Papa Played the Dobro" (Johnny Cash) – 2:55
3 "Boss Jack" (Tex Ritter) – 3:50
4 "Old Doc Brown" (Red Foley) – 4:10

Personnel
Johnny Cash
Luther Perkins: Guitar
Johnny Western: Guitar
Shot Jackson: Dobro, Steel Guitar
Marshall Grant: Bass
Gordon Terry: Fiddle
Floyd Cramer: Piano
Buddy Harman: Drums

OPPOSITE: Johnny Cash during the photo session for the *Ride This Train* album cover. His eighth album was his first concept album. It talked about railroads, how they developed, and how they changed the land, using the train as transport—complete with sound effects—to take the listener on a tour of America, through space and time. The photos were taken by Don Hunstein, a Columbia staff photographer.

LA smog and would come home from school with tears running down her cheeks. By being out of the city this would be alleviated, and being out of public gaze would, it was hoped, calm Johnny down.

Yet if Vivian had expected to enjoy more privacy than at Casitas Springs, she was to be sadly disillusioned; cars would come cruising up the driveway to take a good look at "Johnny Cash's place."

Musically speaking, the singles' success Cash had enjoyed at Sun had initially continued with "All Over Again," and "Don't Take Your Guns To Town." The latter spent six weeks on top of the country charts and was a song that would stay with Cash throughout his career. It would also inspire a string of Western gunslinger tunes and mock-historical sagas by Johnny Horton ("The Battle Of New Orleans"), Marty Robbins ("El Paso"), and Stonewall Jackson ("Waterloo").

Producer Don Law has it that "Don't Take Your Guns To Town" was the song Cash sang to Columbia personnel before he signed in 1958. The single topped the country charts for six weeks and also broke into the *Billboard* Top 40, peaking at #32. The song's poignant tale is of a young cowboy ignoring his mother's advice in an act of youthful recklessness that eventually leads to his demise.

It was noticeable, however, that none of Cash's singles from early 1959 to mid-1963 broke out of the country charts to make it to the *Billboard* pop Top 40. On the long-playing front, *Ride This Train*, recorded in the winter of 1959–1960 and released in September 1960, has been acclaimed one of music's first concept albums thanks to a unique blend of narration and singing.

Cash had long had a fascination with railroads and they often featured in his songs. The new album was subtitled "A Stirring Travelogue of America in Song and Story" and told the tale of life on the rails and was described by some critics as "an education." *Ride This Train* produced a string of Top 20 country hits, the highest-charting, "Come In Stranger,"

reaching #6 despite only clocking in at one and a half minutes long.

Don Law once again joined Cash in the studio and the singer was backed, as always, by the Tennessee Two. Guest musician Shot Jackson doubled up to provide a brilliant performance on steel guitar and Dobro resonator guitar. Bluegrass fiddler Gordon Terry was employed to provide a suitably authentic sound, while acclaimed session pianist and future Country Music Hall of Famer Floyd Cramer gave extra weight to the already stellar cast.

The album began with a narrative piece spoken by Cash where he gives a flavor to the Old West before launching into the opener "Loading Coal," written specially for the project by Kentucky-born guitarist Merle Travis.

Among the highlights is the moving "Dorraine Of Ponchartrain," a Cash-penned saga of lost love that sets the record apart from the somewhat more rigid recordings of the past. The engrossing narrative of "Old Doc Brown" (written by Red Foley of *Ozark Jubilee* TV-show fame) drew the album to a close.

As the 1960s began, Johnny had paid tribute to his influences by recording a batch of tunes made famous by his favorite country singers. The result was the previously mentioned album *Now, There Was A Song!*, on which he covered Bob Wills' "Time Changes Everything." The 1960 release was subtitled "Memories From The Past" and featured a wistful-looking Cash—not quite yet the ubiquitous Man in Black—leaning on a gate resplendent in Stetson and check shirt.

Cash's cover version of George Jones' "Seasons Of My Heart," both opened the album and reached #10 on the *Billboard* country singles chart, while the pace picked up with Kenny Rogers' "I Feel Better Already." Cash channeled the late, great Hank Williams in "I'm So Lonesome I Could Cry," a song later covered by a host of

OPPOSITE and ABOVE: Cash, pictured in 1957, plays up to his Man in Black image, originally devised to make himself and the Tennessee Two look more like a band when they couldn't afford gaudy stage clothes. His early 1970s hit song of the title finally cemented the image.

artists from Bob Dylan to Elvis Presley, who would perform the track on his *Aloha From Hawaii* TV special in 1973.

In 1960 the Tennessee Two had become the Tennessee Three when Perkins and Grant were joined by drummer WS "Fluke" Holland. Holland had been Carl Perkins' drummer for six years and had been present at the Million Dollar Quartet sessions, for which he was paid a princely $11.50 fee. He was originally hired by Cash in 1960 for a run of gigs in New York and Atlantic City. "Those two weeks lasted almost 40 years," he later joked.

Raised in the cotton mill town of Bemis, Tennessee, Holland had never intended to become a drummer. He took a job with an air-conditioning company but used to go to see Carl Perkins and his brothers Clayton and Jay perform at a local club. "I would sometimes walk up to the upright bass and just keep time (with his hands) on the side of the bass on like an uptempo song. I don't know why I did it," Holland explained. "One Saturday night when they were packing up after a gig, Carl said, 'Hey, we got an appointment with Sam Phillips Thursday. Borrow some drums and go with us to Memphis.' "

Johnny's links with the legendary Carter Family, who graced the U.S. airwaves, began with the Family's radio broadcasts which had inspired Johnny when he was growing up in Arkansas. They toured together in the early 1960s and the process culminated in his marrying June Carter in 1968. The summer of 1962 found Cash in Nashville making his first recordings with them. These included folk ("The Legend of John Henry's Hammer") and gospel numbers ("There'll Be Peace In the Valley For Me" and "Were You There When They Crucified My Lord").

Every so often in his career Johnny Cash would release a song or album that would expose him to a new audience. The success of "Ring Of Fire," in 1963, reaching #1 on the

OPPOSITE: Music mogul-to-be Clive Davis, then a CBS Records lawyer and a future label president, looks on as Johnny Cash extends his Columbia contract in 1960, two years after initially signing.

BELOW: Cash and the Tennessee Three perform at 1965's New York City Folk festival. With the Byrds on top of the charts, folk was on trend, and Cash was happy to cash in.

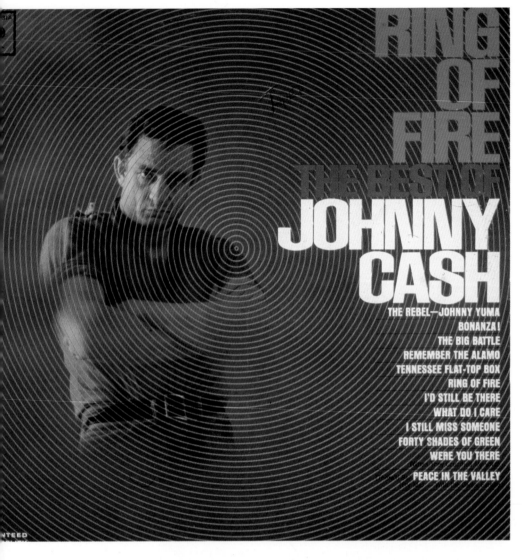

RING
OF
FIRE
THE BEST OF
JOHNNY
CASH

THE REBEL—JOHNNY YUMA
BONANZA!
THE BIG BATTLE
REMEMBER THE ALAMO
TENNESSEE FLAT-TOP BOX
RING OF FIRE
I'D STILL BE THERE
WHAT DO I CARE
I STILL MISS SOMEONE
FORTY SHADES OF GREEN
WERE YOU THERE

PEACE IN THE VALLEY

LEFT: Compilations of his best-known material were regular occurrences in Cash's career. This one was named after his 1963 hit.

OPPOSITE: Merle Kilgore, co-writer of "Ring Of Fire" with either Cash or June Carter, depending on whose account you believe. He was best man at their wedding in 1968.

"Johnny and Merle Kilgore and I were fishing in Casitas, California, and that's when 'Ring Of Fire' was created. After it got pretty well settled, Johnny told Merle Kilgore that this is gonna be one big song. He said, 'I'm going to be going through a divorce, and I don't want it tied up in my divorce, so put June's name down as the writer.'" Vivian Liberto backs up this version of the origins of the song in her book, stating that Cash gave Carter the credit for monetary reasons.

For the recording Cash chose not his usual right-hand man Don Law (though he was in the studio) but returned to Jack Clement, the Sun producer who by now was operating on his own in Beaumont, Texas. Cash had the mold-breaking idea of using trumpets on the recording, not the done thing in Nashville, and needed to work with someone broad-minded enough to share his vision.

The song was originally performed by June's sister, Anita, on her 1963 album *Folk Songs Old and New* as "(Love's) Ring Of Fire." The signature mariachi-style horn arrangement was provided by Cash, who said that it had come to him in a dream. Cash stated, "I'll give you about five or six more months, and if you don't hit with it, I'm gonna record it the way I feel it."

The song, recorded in Nashville with the Carter Family on backing vocals, was Cash's first #1 in four years. It crossed over to the U.S. and UK pop chart and inspired a soundalike follow-up, "The Matador," which made #2 (for two weeks). A "Best Of" collection, also titled *Ring Of Fire*, was the first #1 on *Billboard*'s new Hot Country Albums chart in 1964 and was also Cash's first album to be certified gold by the RIAA.

country charts and entering the Top 20 on the pop listings, was one such record, and brought him to many younger fans who might have been ignorant of his eight-year recording career to that date.

The writing credit combined the names of June Carter and singer-songwriter Merle Kilgore, a distant cousin of the Carter sisters through their maternal grandmother, Margaret Kilgore Addington, but this has been the subject of much debate. In 2007, the *New York Daily News* reported one Curly Lewis, who toured with Cash, as saying that he was present when Cash and Kilgore wrote "Ring of Fire" in a boat.

JOHNNY CASH

LEFT: Cash in unusually light-toned attire.

OPPOSITE: Johnny Cash (center) backstage with bluegrass mandolinist Frank Wakefield (left) and Bob Dylan (right) at the Newport Folk Festival in July 1964 in Newport, Rhode Island.

A second gold album followed hot on its heels with *I Walk The Line*, a country chart-topper for four weeks which also made the pop album charts; it included six new re-recordings of his Sun hits including the title track. As time would show, Cash never quite escaped the shadow of his early pioneering work.

In the mid-1960s, Cash released a number of concept albums as producer Don Law encouraged Cash to branch out in new directions. These included *Ballads Of The True West* (1965), an experimental double album mixing authentic frontier songs with spoken narration, and *Bitter Tears* (1964), with songs highlighting the plight of the Native Americans.

Cash erroneously thought he was descended from Indian ancestry, and empathized with their underdog status. The songs for *Bitter Tears* were written with Peter LaFarge, a New York-based folksinger and songwriter who claimed to be distantly descended from the Narragansett tribe.

But these new directions did not always find favor with country's old guard. In 1964, when his recording of "The Ballad Of Ira Hayes" (about the tragic end suffered by a Native American hero of World War II) received a lukewarm reception on radio, Cash took out a full-page ad in *Billboard* demanding of programers, "Where are your guts?"

Undeterred, Cash continued to broaden his appeal and deepen his creative sources. His appearance at the 1964 Newport Folk Festival, connecting with Bob Dylan at the show, not only added to this but also created a lifelong bond between the two. At first glance, the juxtaposition of Cash and Dylan may seem an odd one. But they had been familiar with each other's work before they met in the early 1960s.

After Cash died in 2003, Dylan wrote: "Of course, I knew of him before he ever heard of me. In 1955 or 1956, 'I Walk The Line' played all summer on the radio, and it was different than anything else you had ever heard. The record sounded like a voice from the middle of the Earth. It was so powerful and moving." When Dylan, nearly ten years his junior, arrived on the scene in 1962, Cash was equally affected. "I was deeply into folk music in the early 1960s," he wrote in his autobiography *Cash*, "both the authentic songs from various periods and areas of American life and the new 'folk revival' songs of the time, so I took note as soon as the *Bob Dylan* album came out in early '62 and listened almost constantly to *The Freewheelin' Bob Dylan* in '63…"

There was also a Dylan connection via the Carter Family, as he'd covered "The Wayworn Traveler" when a young singer-songwriter. His first attempt to add his own words to the melody resulted in "Paths Of Victory," while a change of time signature and lyrics resulted in one of his most famous songs, "The Times They Are A-Changin'." He was following the lead of his hero, Woody Guthrie, who had similarly used the Carters' "When This World's On Fire" as the inspiration for "This Land Is Your Land."

The pair corresponded before they met at the 1964 Newport Folk Festival, where Cash gave Dylan his guitar as a gesture of respect. The pair's friendship remained strong and, in 1969, they would record more than a dozen duets. Only one of them, a version of Dylan's "Girl From The North Country," a song originally performed solo on *The*

Freewheelin' Bob Dylan, was ever officially released, on the album *Nashville Skyline*, although the others have long circulated as bootlegs.

Cash continued his move towards the folk movement when he appeared at the first New York Folk Festival in New York's Carnegie Hall in 1965. His latest album *Orange Blossom Special* — featuring a fiddle tune about the eponomous passenger train — was hailed as "a landmark fusion of C&W and folk," and included "It Ain't Me Babe" and two more Dylan tunes. Meanwhile in mid-1965 he contributed the title song to the John Wayne movie *The Sons Of Katie Elder*.

With folk superstar Bob Dylan on his side, Johnny Cash could eye the future with optimism. He was already taking one foot out of the country category and looking at other opportunities to connect with the wider American record-buying public.

OPPOSITE: Johnny Cash performs at the Newport Folk Festival in July, 1964.

BELOW: Johnny Cash (wearing black) poses for a portrait with "The Brothers Four" (Bob Flick, John Paine, Mike Kirkland and Dick Foley) and film producer and director Sam Katzman (right) in in the early 1960s.

JOHNNY'S GUITARS

Johnny Cash's first decent guitar, bought in Germany and brought back to the United States in 1954, had been the one he strummed when auditioning for Sam Phillips. It survived just three more years before brother Tommy, "horsing around" in Cash's home in Memphis with a nephew, accidentally smashed it. They dared not mention it to him, but fortunately by the time he realized "I didn't care: by then, I had a Martin."

Christian Friedrich Martin had opened his first guitar shop in New York as far back as 1833 and they had already been established as instrument-makers for fifty years by the time Orville Gibson carved his first mandolin. Martin purposely targeted the top end of the market, never exceeding twenty percent of Gibson's output. Its products, made in Nazareth, Pennsylvania and decorated with elaborate inlays, were designed to look as good as they sounded.

Martin had been making square-shouldered "Dreadnoughts"—named after a massive contemporary battleship, as the design was deeper and larger than any of its contemporaries—since 1916. The D-18 and rosewood-bodied D-28 put the D-series on the map in the Thirties, while the D-45 was custom-made for singing cowboy Gene Autry in 1933.

Cash also owned a couple of Fender guitars, but Martin was his preferred brand. Cash liked his guitar so much that, in 1961, he released a song about it. Entitled "Tennessee Flat-Top Box," it made Number 11 on the *Billboard* country chart. Eldest daughter Rosanne recorded it in 1987 for her album *King's Record Shop*, and the result was a #1 country hit.

One of Cash's favorites was a Martin D-41 inlaid with abalone. But his all-time favorite was a specially made D-35, his—and Martin's—first guitar with an all-black finish. This was commissioned when CF Martin III was head of the company and had to be built in secret because CF thought an all-black guitar was "too radical." According to legend, he remained unaware of the instrument until he saw Johnny Cash playing it on *Columbo*. Once he saw it on television, he liked it!

The Man in Black played this guitar on stage for nearly twenty years. Martin later paid tribute to his musical legend with a close facsimile of that special instrument: the D-35 Johnny Cash Commemorative. Its spruce top and rosewood back abalone star fretboard inlays and Johnny Cash signature made it the guitar of choice of the Gaslight Anthem and Mac Powell of Third Day.

Unlike Bob Dylan, Johnny Cash never plugged in and "went electric." Interestingly, daughter Cindy once heard Cash tell a band member that he had never picked up an electric guitar in his life.

OPPOSITE: Assorted guitars, banjos, and memorabilia belonging to Johnny Cash and wife June displayed at Sotheby's on September 7, 2004, in New York. The auction raised almost $4 million including $131,200 for a custom-made Grammer and a black Martin. Cash used this guitar extensively on his television program *The Johnny Cash Show*. Cash gave the guitar to Hank Ballard at the Grand Ole Opry in 1971.

LEFT AND BELOW: Johnny Cash played several brands of guitars throughout his career but his signature black guitar was a specially made D-35, his—and Martin's—first guitar with a polished black finish. Perfect for the Man in Black, Cash played this guitar on stage for nearly 20 years.

OPPOSITE: Cash performs for the ABC-TV cameras.

RIGHT AND FAR RIGHT: A studio portrait of the young Cash; flanked by country duo Johnnie (Wright) and Jack (Anglin).

BELOW: Johnny Cash shows off a personalized guitar.

FAR LEFT: Cash poses with elder statesman of country Ernest Tubb.

LEFT: A contemporary poster.

BELOW: Cash and "Bluebirds Over The Mountain" hitmaker Ersel Hickey listen to a record before going on stage in New York state in February 1959.

OPPOSITE: Sun's two favorite sons, Cash and Presley, pictured together in Memphis in 1967.

Seeing Elvis and other pop stars moving into movies, Cash briefly attempted to become a silver-screen success with 1961's *Five Minutes To Live*. He co-starred in the low-budget effort with Cay Forrester, wife of producer Ludlow Flower Jr. It was re-titled *Door-to-Door Maniac* for a re-release in 1966.

THE OUTLAW 1965–1970

"I love the freedoms we got in this country, I appreciate your freedom to burn your flag if you want to, but I really appreciate my right to bear arms so I can shoot you if you try to burn mine."
Johnny Cash from "Ragged Old Flag" on *The Great Lost Performance*

The 1960s saw Johnny Cash's fame rise, and he has acknowledged the decade as "probably my most productive time, creatively speaking." Away from stage and studio, however, his excessive behavior persisted. The period Johnny and Vivian Cash and their four girls spent in Ventura County from 1961 to 1967 would bring pills and booze, binges, and arrests—not to mention a forest fire.

"Ojai [the name of his house near Lake Casitas, California] means to nest," he observed, adding that "nesting wasn't what I did." Touring was what he did. And he wasn't going to give up on that. The amphetamines were countered by alcohol, "to take off the edge," and he eventually got into barbituates. The temper he inherited from his father, Ray, could strike at any time. In 1965, in a fit of rage, he smashed the floor lights at the Grand Ole Opry, resulting in a long-standing ban.

Thus it was that Cash was "full of amphetamines and arrogance" when, in June 1965, he faced charges for starting a forest fire that devastated several hundred acres in Los Padres National Forest. It happened when his camper van with black-painted windows caught fire, apparently due to oil seeping from a cracked bearing.

Strange as it may seem, Cash may have exaggerated the incident to enhance his outlaw credentials. Accounts from the time said he was fined about $125,000, but a newspaper later reported it was reduced to about $82,000 and that Cash's insurance companies were ordered to pick up the tab.

In his 1997 autobiography, he recalled the incident in his inimitable style. He said he went into a later court proceeding refusing to answer questions and denied starting the fire, apparently saying, "No, my truck did and it's dead, so you can't question it."

He also said that the fire, close to a sanctuary, scared off or killed forty-four California condors. Asked about that in a deposition, Cash wrote that he replied, "don't give a damn about your yellow buzzards." However, the U.S. Fish and Wildlife Service said if any condors had died, there would have been a record. Dennis Ensign, a firefighter who fought the blaze, recalled no dead birds. So maybe Johnny Cash was happy to give himself a little more of a rebellious image than he deserved.

However, when it came to drugs, no exaggeration was needed. In October 1965, he was arrested by a narcotics squad in El Paso. Instead of the heroin officers suspected he was smuggling from Mexico, Cash's guitar case was found to contain 688 Dexedrine capsules and 475 Equanil tablets the singer had hidden. Because the pills were prescription drugs rather than illegal narcotics, he received a suspended sentence. Underlying Johnny Cash's gradual discovery of his talent as an artist was lack of self-esteem and a need to prove himself, to himself and to his father. This led to his drinking, drug-taking, and womanizing, resulting in degradation and despair.

As far as the movie *Walk The Line* (2005) was concerned, Cash hit rock bottom but was saved by the love of a good

ABOVE: Cash's police mugshot after being caught with prescription drugs in his guitar case when re-entering the States from Mexico, October 1965.

woman. June Carter had grown up in the country music business as a member of a family of star performers and had some understanding of the pressure Cash was under. It's an over-simplification, of course, but June Carter would indeed play a major role in the second half of Cash's life story.

Their marriage cemented a friendship that dated back to when Johnny had encountered the Carter Family. He'd first set eyes on June in 1950 when he was still at Dyess High School; the class had a trip booked to the Grand Ole Opry, and June, three years his senior, was performing. "She was great. She was gorgeous. She was a star. I was smitten," he wrote in his second autobiography.

Six years later, in 1956, he set eyes on her again. The venue was still the Grand Ole Opry, but this time they were both performing. "You and I are going to get married someday," the still-smitten Cash had declared—but the timing had clearly not been right. He was still married to Vivian; she was married to honky-tonk singer Carl Smith. In late 1961, Cash's manager Saul Holiff booked June as a support act for a big show, and the following year had seen her join the Cash roadshow as a permanent fixture.

The pair's relationship, not surprisingly, deepened and the writing was soon on the wall for his first marriage. Daughter Cindy: "Once June came along, she relentlessly— well, she wanted Dad and she was going to get him. And she did. She made herself very available, to (the point) where he pursued her back."

Twice-married June went into the relationship with her eyes wide open. She once said of her future husband that there were two men inside him: "John the caring family man and Cash the selfish bastard."

Born in a remote valley in Virginia in 1929, she had been a professional musician ever since, as a child radio performer, she sang alongside her sisters Helen and Anita and her mother Maybelle. Maybelle was a member of the Carter Family, the first group to make it big in country music, with Alvin Pleasant "AP" Carter and his wife Sara (Maybelle's first cousin). Sara sang lead and played autoharp, while Maybelle added harmony as well as uniquely playing the melody on the bass strings of her guitar.

Maybelle's ability to keep the rhythm going on the higher strings while doing this would prove influential on such famous flatpickers that followed as Doc Watson, Clarence White, and Norman Blake. Before the Carter Family's recordings, the guitar had rarely been used as a lead or solo instrument by white musicians. The combination of a melodic line on the bass strings with intermittent strumming is now a staple of the steel-string guitarist's repertoire.

The Carter Family had reached a new audience in the late 1930s via border radio station XERA which, broadcasting from Mexico, was unregulated by authorities in the States and thus had a far more powerful and wide-ranging signal than its competitors. As well as Johnny Cash in Arkansas, Waylon Jennings in Texas, Chet Atkins in Georgia, and Tom T. Hall in Kentucky all eagerly listened to and learned from them.

AP and Sara bowed out after the Carter Family did their last radio show together in 1942, but Maybelle recruited Helen, Anita, and June to keep the tradition going. The girls also performed on their own as the more modern-sounding Carter Sisters.

At the age of fourteen, June claimed she saw tongues of fire on the day of Pentecost and believed the Holy Spirit entered her body. Her Christian faith was one of the most important elements in her life.

In 1952, June married Carl Smith, with whom she performed at the Grand Ole Opry and had a daughter, Rebecca Carlene. After their divorce, she toured with Elvis Presley and was briefly married to police officer Edwin "Rip" Nix, with whom she had another daughter, Rosie.

In the mid-1950s, June studied at the Actor's Studio in New York City, landing a movie role in 1958's *Country Music Holiday*, as well as guest spots on TV

RIGHT: Cash pictured with his future wife June Carter (left) and future mother-in-law Maybelle Carter (center).

BELOW: Group shot of American country and folk music pioneers, the Carter family, in 1941 in Poor Valley, Virginia (L–R): Gladys Carter Millard, Sara, Flo Millard (front), Ezra, Maybelle, Anita, Margaret Addington, Helen, June, Joe, and A.P. Gladys and Joe were two of A.P. and Sara's three children (Jett missing from photo). Helen, June, and Anita were children of Ezra J. Carter and Maybelle Addington Carter.

westerns and soap operas. But she returned to music with her mother and sisters in the early 1960s to work with Johnny Cash.

Back home in Ojai, all was not sweetness and light in the Cash family nest. It had been difficult for Vivian to bring up their daughters single-handed. Her hard-touring husband had not been home to share in birthdays, celebrations, school prizegivings, and the like, and his pill-fueled lifestyle had

meant that, by his own admission, he'd not even maintained telephone communication to an acceptable degree. "She'd say, 'If I only could have traveled with him instead of being here raising four kids, things would have been different,' " recalled Vivian's long-time friend Alice Smith.

Vivian finally filed for divorce from Johnny in summer 1966; it was granted in late 1967. After signing the divorce papers, she said she still had hope. She called him on tour

and asked if there was any chance of reconciliation. Cash declined, replying simply, "No, it's too late."

But his desire to get together with June Carter foundered on the other love of his life—pills. Johnny would promise time and again to kick his habit but he always relapsed. Even when he bought an apartment in Nashville in order to be closer to her, he shared it with legendary hellraiser Waylon Jennings, and the two egged each other on in their drug-taking.

To the record-buying public, however, Johnny and June seemed already very much in harmony. Having successfully duetted with June on Bob Dylan's "It Ain't Me Babe" in 1967, their next joint effort "Jackson" (with Carl Perkins on guitar) made #2 on the country chart; a quick cover by Nancy Sinatra and Lee Hazlewood was a pop hit three months later, but the original won its performers a Grammy Award in 1968 for Best Country & Western Performance Duet, Trio or Group. It was also a standout of the 2005 movie *Walk The Line* when performed by Joaquin Phoenix and Reese Witherspoon.

September 1967 brought Johnny and June's first jointly recorded album. *Carryin' On With Johnny Cash & June Carter* not only reprised their chart duets but also added others including two from Ray Charles, "I Got a Woman" and "What'd I Say."

As well as harmonizing on stage and in the studio, June was now playing a major role in Cash's private life. And this took time to settle down. His final drug-related arrest in 1967 in Walker County, Georgia, led to a night in LaFayette jail. The singer, who was involved in a car accident while

OPPOSITE: Johnny Cash rehearses with his wife Vivian Liberto for his upcoming appearance on the television show Ranch Party.

ABOVE RIGHT: Country singers Johnny Cash and June Carter pose for a portrait.

RIGHT: Johnny and June on stage in Los Angeles in 1968, the year they married.

carrying a bag of prescription pills, was released after Sheriff Ralph Jones warned him of his dangerous behavior and wasted potential. Cash later came back to LaFayette to play a benefit concert that raised $75,000 for the local high school.

In October 1967 June's intervention reportedly prevented Johnny from taking his own life. He'd canceled countless gigs and recording sessions during the year, while the pills he was taking dried out his throat so badly he often couldn't sing when he did show up. Maddened by his increasing drug intake, he headed for Nickajack Cave in Chattanooga, near the Tennessee River, and crawled inside, hoping he might be put out of his misery.

He knew the cave from going there to search for Civil War and Native American artifacts, and he was well acquainted with the fact that many cave explorers had died deep inside Nickajack's byzantine architecture.

"The absolute lack of light was appropriate," he'd later reflect, "for at that moment I was as far from God as I have ever been. My separation from Him, the deepest and most ravaging of the various kinds of loneliness I'd felt over the years, seemed finally complete."

Although he admitted God didn't speak to him—"He never has, and I'll be very surprised if He ever does"—he decided to crawl back to the mouth of the cave, where June and his mother were waiting for him with a basket of food, and confront his demons. Apparently Carrie Cash "knew something was wrong" and had flown all the way from California to find her beloved son and help him.

It should be noted that author Robert Hilburn has cast doubt on this story. His 2013 biography *Johnny Cash: The Life* notes that the cave would have been underwater on the day Cash often cited, and that the singer still used drugs afterwards. Whatever the truth, a month later he played his first concert "straight" for a decade, in Hendersonville, and life was about to take an upturn again.

His personal life had been a mess of his own making. While a religious and moral man, he battled drugs daily. He'd left his first wife, a Catholic, for June Carter who, when they first met, was married to his buddy Carl Smith. Yet all these ups and downs added to his ability to plumb the depths of his psyche for performances that stirred the soul; he recognized this when he said "I've always felt there's a war going on inside of me…good fighting against evil." There must be redemption, though, he concludes, "or I wouldn't be here."

In February 1968 Cash proposed to June onstage at the London Ice House, a hockey arena in London, Ontario. He chose his moment to do so in the middle of a performance of "Jackson." She accepted, and they married a week later.

He described how she stuck with him through years of amphetamine abuse in his 1997 autobiography. "June said she knew me—knew the kernel of me, deep inside, beneath the drugs and deceit and despair and anger and selfishness, and knew my loneliness," he wrote. "She said she could help me… If she found my pills, she flushed them down the toilet. And find them she did—she searched for them, relentlessly."

June and Johnny moved into the idyllic lakeside house he'd bought near Nashville, and life from then on would be very different for both of them. She moved both her daughters into Cash's house and her stepdaughters and parents were always made welcome.

June loved being Johnny's wife, even though their life together held many surprises. Once he told her that twenty-four people would be coming for lunch. Instead, seventy-six showed up. And while the house had been sparsely furnished when Cash lived there alone, June, who had a mania for collecting furniture, filled it with period pieces, while staff attended the couple's every whim.

Johnny and June married on March 1, 1968. He'd already played his legendary Fulsom Prison show that year, and a new television series was soon confirmed to start in 1969.

OPPOSITE: Carter and Cash's on-stage double act not only got them into the charts with "Jackson" but also won them a Grammy.

Last, but far from least, June bore Johnny his first and only son, John Carter Cash, on March 3, 1970. His faith had seen him through this time—but it was a close-run thing.

There was still time to register one final country chart-topper in 1968. "Daddy Sang Bass," with its writer Carl Perkins on guitar and The Statler Brothers and Carter Family on background vocals, stayed at #1 for six weeks. It was taken from *The Holy Land*, an album of songs about Israel. The lyric mentioned Cash's "little brother" Jack, who had died so tragically in their youth.

Luther Perkins of the Tennessee Three was also to die before his time, the apparent victim of a 1968 house fire. It was suggested he fell asleep on a couch with a cigarette in his hand, though this was never confirmed. He was replaced by Bob Wootton, a guitarist who had studied the Three and could play Luther's licks note for note. "He came as close as any man could," said Cash, "to filling the hole Luther had left." Cash missed his long-time right-hand man who "shared that edge of nervousness" with him. But the music would carry on.

The spring of 1969 saw Johnny and June make a pilgrimage to Vietnam, where the United States was fighting an unwinnable war against communism. The draft had been taking thousands of young men to fight in

LEFT: Johnny Cash performs onstage with guitarist Carl Perkins in 1968 in Los Angeles, California.

OPPOSITE: Bob Wootton took the place of Luther Perkins in the Tennessee Three after his predecessor's untimely death in a 1968 house fire.

a conflict few believed in, and Cash, while a patriot, was appalled by what he saw and the tales he heard.

The couple played music at night and visited the field hospitals during the day. It was an experience that affected them greatly, and inspired songs like "Man In Black." Kathy Cash later revealed that "When he went to Vietnam it really hit him—it really got to him. He was so upset when he came back; he talked about men that had shrapnel in them, and [how] they had used Agent Orange, and all these things that he was just horribly baffled by, and he really became more vocal about it. He saw first-hand what kind of harm and damage it was doing."

From 1969 to 1971, Cash starred in his own television show, *The Johnny Cash Show*, on the ABC network (see pages 126–135). The roll-call of guests ranged from

early influences like Ray Charles and Louis Armstrong to contemporary performers he rated highly like Joni Mitchell and Linda Ronstadt. He also made a point of spotlighting country musicians who could not usually break out of their market, allowing them exposure to the mainstream.

Bob Dylan, a prestigious guest on the first show, was emerging from a reclusive period following his 1966 motorcycle crash. Nearly ten years Johnny's junior, he looked on him as a father figure; Cash, for his part, inherited Dylan's producer Bob Johnston.

Artists who received a major career boost from *The Johnny Cash Show* included Kenny Rogers, whose First Edition appeared a record four times, James Taylor, Derek and the Dominos (featuring Eric Clapton), and Kris Kristofferson, who was beginning to make a name for

himself as a singer/songwriter. Cash refused to change the lyrics of Kristofferson's "Sunday Mornin' Comin' Down" to suit network executives, singing the song with soft-drug references intact.

The unhappy powers that be were also unimpressed when Cash made direct references to his Christian faith on air. After one head-to-head with his producer, he stated he had no intentions of shutting up, stating: "If you don't like it, you can always edit it." Nothing more was said. Ironically, the shows were staged at the Ryman Auditorium, a converted church that had been home to the Grand Ole Opry since 1943.

Producing the show was taking a big chunk of Cash's working week, from Monday when preparations began to Thursday when the show was filmed. He would insist on playing concerts for the rest of the week, which left precious little down time. At least June was with him on the tour bus, but he admitted he was relieved when ABC decided to end the show after its second series.

Johnny Cash's career was full of contradictions. In terms of his popularity, he sold more records than The Beatles in 1969, but as time went by he would find it impossible to get radio airplay in his own country. The many musical revolutions that had transformed the 1960s scene had made solo stars passé, and Cash was not immune to that.

He may have been losing his place on the airwaves, but Johnny Cash was by no means finished. He would face the challenges of a new decade, the 1970s, with wife June steadfastly by his side.

OPPOSITE: Publicity still from TV's *The Johnny Cash Show*, which ran from 1969–1971 on the ABC network.

RIGHT: Cash in the studio in 1969.

OPPOSITE: Johnny Cash in his dressing room at the Hammersmith Odeon, before playing a London show in 1966. He would not play the venue again until 1983, having graduated to the larger Albert Hall.

ABOVE LEFT: Johnny and June pass through London's Heathrow Airport in 1968. Their British following was loyal and fast-growing, and had been since his first TV appearance on *Boy Meets Girl* in 1959.

ABOVE RIGHT: Backstage at the Hammersmith Odeon, where cigarettes were clearly still permitted in 1966. Cash was an inveterate smoker throughout his life.

LEFT: Cash smiles as he poses with three Scottish bagpipers in a promotional still for his television special, *Johnny Cash: Christmas in Scotland*, November 13, 1981.

RIGHT: Cash performing on stage at the Wembley Arena Festival of Country Music in 1986.

ABOVE: Johnny Cash chats with some of the inmates and guests during his visit to Cummins Prison in Arkansas. April 10, 1969.

OPPOSITE: Cash enters the gates of Folsom Prison, preparing to perform his fourth concert for inmates there; California, 1964.

Two major prison concert recordings brought Johnny Cash's 1960s to a triumphant end, bringing him his first U.S. chart-topping album. Cash had been playing "behind bars" since 1956, but it was his appearances at Folsom and San Quentin prisons in 1968 and 1969 that gave his career a boost and cemented his outlaw image—this despite the fact that he had never served a jail term.

He was passionate about penal reform, as his son John Carter Cash emphasized when he co-produced a reissue of the Folsom set: "He knew that he was singing for murderers, rapists, and killers but he also knew that he was singing for people that were suffering greater hardships than they were due."

This excerpt from the original liner notes to the *At Folsom Prison* album gives a taste of Cash's passion: "The culture of a thousand years is shattered with the clanging of the cell door behind you. Life outside behind you immediately becomes unreal. You begin to not care that it exists. All you have with you in the cell is your bare animal instincts."

Two concerts were taped at California's Folsom Prison in January 1968 and released that summer. June Carter, Carl Perkins, and the Tennessee Three backed Cash, with fifteen tracks from the first show and two tracks from the second making up the album as originally released.

The concert was introduced by a rendition of his classic "Folsom Prison Blues," originally cut for Sun. Issued as a single, a live version of the song was a Top 40 US hit, Cash's first since 1964's "Understand Your Man." Another highlight of the album was "Dark As A Dungeon," written by singer-songwriter Merle Travis and a rallying cry for miners seeking improved conditions.

Cash's concept for this record was to create a concert of prison-related songs to play to a crowd of prisoners. As one critic has since marveled, "A concept record was one thing but a live concept record conjured up explicitly for the people who are supposedly at the bottom of society's barrel? In many ways, *At Folsom Prison* was a bolder, more

daring album than The Beatles' fawned-over masterwork (*Sgt Pepper*)."

Marshall Grant recalled that it was a "somber atmosphere…(there was) no joy here," while an accompanying reporter later admitted to being, "a little nervous." And little wonder: some prisoners had taken a guard hostage two weeks before, and tension was in the air. The governor told the inmates that if anyone left their chair during the concert they would stop the show, and there were guards with loaded rifles on walkways above the stage.

Carl Perkins and The Statler Brothers warmed up the crowd before disc jockey Hugh Cherry came out to advise the 1,000-strong audience in the prison dining room that the show was going to be recorded. They were to hold their applause until Cash gave his signature greeting, "Hello, I'm Johnny Cash"—and the assembled crowd of hardened criminals were happy to oblige.

One of the songs he played, "Greystone Chapel," was written by Folsom inmate Glen Sherley, whose career as a country and western singer after his release was supported and nurtured by Johnny Cash.

Cash's first LP with new producer Bob Johnston soared to #13 in the States, where it spent two years on the chart, and #8 in the UK (53 weeks). It was certified platinum and chosen as CMA Album of the Year in October. The album

was re-released with additional tracks in 1999 and as a three-disc set in 2008. It was certified triple platinum in 2003 by the Recording Industry Association of America for U.S. sales exceeding three million.

Having created a best-seller behind prison walls, Columbia repeated the trick the following year, recording a second set at San Quentin Prison in February—the month before *Folsom Prison Blues* won a Grammy. This was for Best Country Vocal Performance, Male (a second, less expected win came in the category of Best Liner Notes).

It was Cash's fourth show at San Quentin; his first, in 1957, had found 22-year old inmate Merle Haggard sitting in the first row. The song "Starkville City Jail" was inspired by

OPPOSITE: 26 July 1972. Johnny Cash as he testified on prison reform before Senate subcommittee on national penitentiaries. At left is Senator Bill Brock of Tennessee.

ABOVE: Cash signs autographs after arriving in Atlanta to do a show for prisoners connected with the early release program. At right is Walker County Sheriff Ralph Jones, who in 1967 inspired Cash to "change his ways" when the singer was detained overnight in his jail.

OPPOSITE AND LEFT: An episode of *The Johnny Cash Show* was filmed in April 1969 at Cummins Prison in Arkansas, generally thought to be the worst prison in the state. During his performance, Cash pledged $5,000 of his own money to build a chapel, and challenged Governor Winthrop Rockefeller to match his pledge. The chapel built as a result of that donation (and the governor's matching check) remains today, a testament to Cash's concern for the spiritual life of those behind bars.

his May 1965 arrest in Starkville, Mississippi, for trespassing late at night onto private property to pick flowers. The event was not only recorded for a live album but also filmed for a British TV documentary by TV company Granada.

The *San Quentin* record included the crossover hit single "A Boy Named Sue," a novelty song penned by Shel Silverstein. The lyricist, most famed for Dr. Hook's "Sylvia's Mother," had delivered the song to Cash a few days earlier, and it was so new he had to have the lyrics written out to refer to.

The song, about a young man dedicated to wreaking revenge on his father for giving him a woman's name, connected with the public just as it did with the convicts. It reached #1 on the country charts and #2 on the U.S. pop Top 10 when extracted from the album, an edited version without bad language was specially prepared for radio.

Cash had also debuted a new song named after the jail. The bitter lyrics, written from the point of view of the inmates ("San Quentin, I hate every inch of you") nearly sparked a riot. "The prisoners stood up on the tables and stomped their feet," he later recalled. "They demanded that I sing it again, which I did. We were all a little uneasy, because they were really overly excited."

Yet Cash had never felt threatened. "Maybe I should have, but I always felt safe. I felt that the inmates would have protected me as much as the guards did." As well as responding to his songs of rebellion, they had reacted passionately to "Peace In The Valley," a spiritual also recorded by Elvis Presley that was included on the album but for some reason was not listed on its sleeve.

And the music didn't finish after his last encore. As Cash took his leave of San Quentin, he responded to requests from the convicts on Death Row and, taking his guitar from its case and laying it on the pavement outside the prison, busked his way through "Folsom Prison Blues" as a special treat.

The album, which kicked off with Bob Dylan's "Wanted Man," entered the country charts, which it headed for an amazing twenty weeks, and spent four weeks at #1 in the pop listings—Cash's first and only U.S. chart-topping LP. It was certified double platinum, was chosen as Country Music Association Album of the Year and won Cash the CMA Entertainer Of the Year award.

At San Quentin deposed the original cast recording of the hippie musical *Hair*, which had ruled for thirteen weeks. The contrast could not have been starker, and said much about the eclectic nature of music in the 1960s.

Cash, who would play one final (unrecorded) concert at Folsom in 1977, ultimately gave up lobbying for reform and had stopped doing prison shows by the end of the decade. His daughter Rosanne felt he was frustrated by the lack of progress, believing, "It was too much of a burden."

Even so, Cash's prison albums remain landmarks in both country music and his own career.

BELOW AND OPPOSITE: August 13, 1970, saw Johnny Cash and June Carter, play a benefit concert organized by Lafayette, Georgia's business community. The show, in a sports stadium, drew thousands of people, but these pictures are of a special performance played earlier that day to about 600 men on an early-release plan from Atlanta State Prison. Cash also made a motivational speech.

MADISON SQUARE GARDEN

Shots from Johnny Cash concerts at New York's Madison Square Garden in 1970 (OPPOSITE) and 1969. The latter show was recorded for a live album, which was not released until 2002. The delay was due to the fact that Cash's seminal *At San Quentin* album had only just appeared.

As with all Cash live shows of this period, he was backed by the Tennessee Three, The Statler Brothers, Carl Perkins, his brother Tommy and the Carter Family. Cash also introduced his father Ray from the stage, as well as Shel Silverstein, who wrote "A Boy Named Sue."

Billboard review of the 1969 show noted: "A tuxedo-clad Johnny Cash must have cut an imposing figure when he took the stage at New York's Madison Square Garden in December 1969, performing songs about prison, cocaine, and murder alongside gospel hymns and patriotic antiwar sentiments (as a self-proclaimed 'dove with claws'). As this uncovered gem from Columbia/Legacy demonstrates, the MSG sellout crowd responded with enthusiasm and a bit of awe, from the opening twangs and the 'Hello, I'm Johnny Cash' greeting through a monster twenty-six-song classic set. Cash was a major star, with his personal demons largely in control and a major network TV series in full swing. He was also a commanding onstage presence despite the strain a heavy touring schedule put on his voice… This is Cash's stage, and he owns it."

THE MAN IN BLACK 1970–1989

"I wore black because I liked it. I still do, and wearing it still means something to me. It's still my symbol of rebellion—against a stagnant status quo, against our hypocritical houses of God, against people whose minds are closed to others' ideas."

Johnny Cash

The 1970s started promisingly when Johnny and June's duet of Tim Hardin's "If I Were A Carpenter" hit #2 on the country and #36 on the pop charts. The album on which it appeared, *Hello, I'm Johnny Cash* (after his customary stage greeting to the audience), hit the top of the *Billboard* country chart and was certified gold. It made the #6 position in both the UK and U.S. pop listings in the slipstream of the U.S. chart-topping *At San Quentin*.

The 1970 Grammies saw Johnny walk away with two awards: "A Boy Named Sue" won for Best Country Vocal Performance, Male, while, less expectedly, his sleeve notes for Bob Dylan's *Nashville Skyline* album also won an award. "If I Were a Carpenter" was just too late to be eligible but belatedly won a Grammy for Best Country Performance by a Duo/Group at the 13th annual awards in 1971. It would be Cash's last such recognition for more than fifteen years.

Johnny Cash the all-American icon was invited to play the White House in April 1970 by President Nixon. It's a fair bet that Nixon, no great music fan, was instructed it would be good for his popularity to associate himself with Cash. He asked him to play two recently popular country songs, Merle Haggard's "Okie From Muskogee" and Guy Drake's "Welfare Cadillac." Cash respectfully declined, and played his own "A Boy Named Sue" which had also been requested. "One thing I've learned about Johnny Cash," Nixon joked in his introduction, "is that you don't tell him what to sing."

Cash's late-1970 album *The Johnny Cash Show* was recorded live at the Grand Ole Opry and was a country chart-topper for four weeks. The single that preceded it was Kris Kristofferson's "Sunday Morning Coming Down," the song written from the point of view of a drug addict he had premiered on his TV show. It too hit #1 in the country listing and would win its writer the prestigious CMA Song of the Year award.

Though it's little remembered now in the wake of the posthumous bio-pic of the same name, a movie called *I Walk The Line* premiered in 1970. Based on the novel *An Exile* by Madison Jones, it starred Gregory Peck as a small-town sheriff and Tuesday Weld as the girl from across the tracks he fell for. Cash re-recorded the title song for the movie, and ended up with enough material for a soundtrack album. Both this and a single, "Flesh And Blood," entered the country charts; the LP hit #9 and the single #1 in 1971.

Johnny Cash officially become the "Man In Black" in early 1971, when the song of that name was written. One of its first—maybe its first ever—performance was in front of an all-student audience at the Ryman Auditorium in Nashville. The song was so new when he performed it for the TV special called *Johnny Cash On Campus*, which aired in February 1971, that he needed cue cards to prompt him!

The Kent State shootings, in which the National Guard had slain four unarmed demonstrating students,

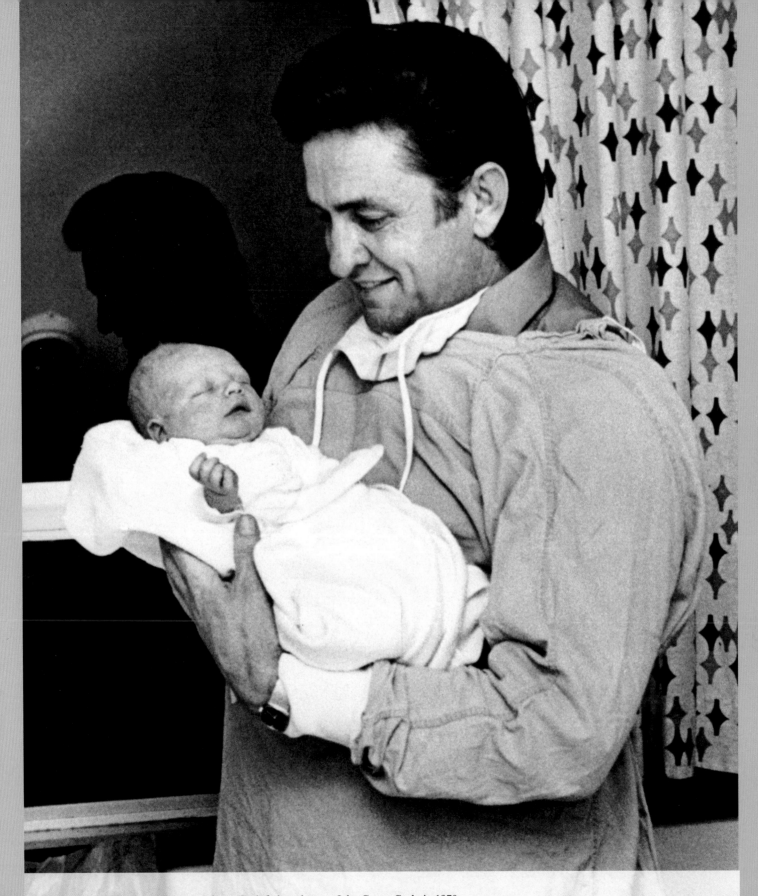

Four times a father to daughters; Johnny Cash fathered a son, John Carter Cash, in 1970.

had happened the year before, and 1971 was a time of widespread demonstrations over the Vietnam War and other issues. "Man In Black," perhaps the ultimate protest song, reached across generations and appealed to audiences much wider than those usually afforded country music.

The lyrics of the song, he explained in his live introduction, came from a visit made few days earlier to the campus of nearby Vanderbilt University. "You asked me questions, I asked you questions, and an idea for a song started brewing."

"It's a very personal thing but it's the way I feel about a lot of things." His lyrics stood up for "the poor and the beaten down," "the prisoner who has long paid for his crime," unbelievers, the "sick and lonely old," drug addicts and those who died in Vietnam. The line "each week we lose a hundred fine young men" received an ovation.

His last producer Rick Rubin later defined the Man in Black character as "Someone who's haunted and remorseful, who wrestles with demons, but it seems with him like the demons win most of the time. He always

OPPOSITE: The Man in Black— Johnny Cash TV show Copenhagen September 1971. In the background, Carl Perkins.

RIGHT: The Nixons and the Cashes at the White House.

BELOW: President Nixon discovers Johnny is not about to sing "Okie From Muskogee" at his White House concert, 1970.

has to live with the darkness of what he's done, he never gets off scot-free, which aligns him with the prisoners, the outlaws, of the world."

May 1971 saw the final broadcast of *The Johnny Cash Show*, though he returned to the small screen in August 1976 when, taped at the Grand Ole Opry, it returned for four weeks as a summer replacement variety series on CBS-TV.

As TV commitments ended, Johnny and June headed for Israel to film *Gospel Road*, a documentary about contemporary life in the Holy Land. The soundtrack contained some songs by Larry Gatlin, one of a number of young country artists he patronized. The end of the year saw him rack up his final platinum album for some years to come in *The Johnny Cash Collection*, a second volume of greatest hits.

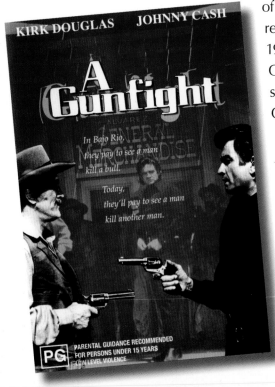

His concentration on *Gospel Road* led Cash to make a decision he would rue for the rest of his life: he turned down the chance to record Steve Goodman's train song "City Of New Orleans," which became a classic in the hands of Arlo (son of Woody) Guthrie. But Cash described the 1970s in general as a decade of "abundance and growth," while recognizing that his recording career was in decline.

It wasn't surprising, then, that he decided to diversify his activities. While he would continue touring and recording, an increasingly important part of Cash's life was acting in movies and on television. He starred alongside Kirk Douglas in the Western *A Gunfight*, while March 1972 saw him make a guest appearance opposite Ida Lupino on TV detective show *Columbo*.

Another small-screen appearance in the 1970s found him singing "Five Feet High And Rising" on TV's *Sesame Street*. The character Biff with whom he shared the screen dramatically stacked foot-high blocks to represent each foot the song's waters rose, but the song ended not with dead bodies but with Cash advising children to learn how to swim.

Other television appearances in the years to come would include an episode of *Little House on the Prairie*, with wife June, and the 1985 American Civil War television mini-series *North And South* in which he played John Brown.

He was also involved with the TV series *Dr Quinn Medicine Woman*, a vehicle for British actress Jane Seymour which ran from 1993 to 1998. (The actress thought so highly of Cash that she later named one of her twin sons after him.) He played retired gunfighter Kid Cole, while June was his screen wife Ruth McKenzie—initially in an episode called *Saving Souls*, the characters proved so popular they appeared in several more episodes.

OPPOSITE: *A Gunfight* saw Cash starring opposite Kirk Douglas.

ABOVE: Cash with Larry Gatlin.

RIGHT: A moment of reflection at Jerusalem's Western Wall while filming a Christmas TV special in Israel, 1977.

Cash's records were notably selling in greater quantities in the United Kingdom (where he'd toured in the summer of 1971) than at home. An example was the single "A Thing Called Love," which saw him backed by the Evangel Temple Choir. In Britain this made #4 as a single and the identically named album #8, while the LP stalled at #112 on the *Billboard* listing. Columbia swiftly whipped a compilation together and *Star Portrait* followed it into the UK Top 20 as Christmas approached.

The year ended with *Johnny Cash: America (A 200-year Salute In Story And Song)*, a concept LP with narrative interwoven between new and previously issued "period" songs. This again disappointed chartwise, stalling at a lowly U.S. #176.

The soundtrack to 1971's *Gospel Road* documentary featuring the Carter Family, was finally released in 1973, the year Cash shared a stage with evangelist Billy Graham and British pop idol Cliff Richard at London's Wembley Stadium. Witnessing his religion in public fashion was an important element of his life. Billy Graham would become a firm friend and house guest in Jamaica. "I have never known a greater man among men," said Cash of his friend.

OPPOSITE AND RIGHT: Cash's return to the big screen in 1971 was a Western called *A Gunfight* opposite Kirk Douglas (and here, Karen Black). It was relatively low-key with the pair playing Will Tenneray and Abe Cross, two aging gunfighters, both in need of money. The movie was financed by the Jicarilla Apache Tribe, although there are no leading Native American characters in the story.

The House Of Cash recording studio was now in full operation, and releases recorded there included all members of the family: his forty-sixth album, *Johnny Cash And His Woman*, naturally featured June, while his forty-eighth *The Junkie and the Juicehead Minus Me* marked the recording debuts of two teenagers, stepdaughter Carlene Carter and eldest daughter Rosanne Cash.

The year of 1975 brought Cash's first autobiography, inevitably titled *The Man In Black*. It was arguably a suitable year in which to reflect on life and mortality; major country figures Lefty Frizzell, Cousin Jody, George Morgan, Audrey Williams (Hank Williams' widow) and promoter Oscar Davis all died in that calendar year while Marty Robbins, Lester Flatt, Earl Scruggs, Hank Williams Jr, and Elvis Presley all spent time in hospital.

It was a miserable time all round; the music business as a whole was suffering from the effects of the oil crisis which both curtailed touring and restricted record pressing, oil being a vital ingredient of vinyl. But June 1976 brought better news.

The album *One Piece At A Time*, on which he shared billing with the Tennessee Three, would prove his biggest in four years thanks to the success of the title song.

OPPOSITE: Cash sings for Danish TV in September 1971. The nineteen-song performance, which included duets with June Carter and contributions from Carl Perkins and The Statler Brothers, was released as *Johnny Cash In Denmark* in 2006, three years after his death.

RIGHT: The Man in Black with "Rhinestone Cowboy" Glen Campbell on his television show, 1972.

Written by little-known Oklahoman country singer Wayne Kemp and describing a worker in a car plant building his own vehicle from stolen parts, it would be denigrated in some quarters as a novelty. Nevertheless it became Cash's last country chart-topper and, unusually, did better in the U.S. pop chart than the UK, making #29 and #32 respectively.

The joke was that it took the thief over twenty-four years to build the car—so when Bruce Fitzpatrick, owner of Abernathy Auto Parts and Hilltop Auto Salvage in Nashville was asked to build the vehicle for international promotion, he had to ensure he had all the models of Cadillacs mentioned in the song in stock. The result, presented to Johnny in April 1976, was parked outside the House Of Cash in Hendersonville, Tennessee, until a place was found to store it. The whole affair must have brought back memories of his own brief spell in the auto assembly business over two decades previously.

1976 was The United States' bicentennial year, and Johnny Cash was very much in the thick of the celebrations. He gave a concert at the Washington Monument, and then came off stage to ring a replica of the Liberty Bell, a gift from the United Kingdom, as red, white, and blue fireworks filled the sky.

The fourth annual American Music Awards honored Johnny with its special Award of Merit in January 1977. Albums and singles included *The Last Gunfighter Ballad* (with the title track a successful single) and *The Rambler*, with associated singles "Lady" and "After The Ball." The

ABOVE LEFT: Cash performs live with June Carter in Amsterdam, Holland in 1972.

LEFT: Johnny and June Carter pose in Berlin on July 24, 1972.

OPPOSITE: Cash pictured at Heathrow airport with his wife June Carter and their eighteen-month-old son John in September 1971.

OPPOSITE: Johnny and June posed together in the back seat of their limousine in Amsterdam, Holland in 1972.

ABOVE: Johnny Cash and June Carter arrived in Australia with their son John Carter Cash on March 19, 1973.

following year brought three albums, *Itchy Feet, Gone Girl*, and *I Would Like To See You Again*, but only the first-named, subtitled "20 Foot-Tapping Greats," made a major impact, nosing four places into the UK Top 40.

British fans were rewarded in March 1979 with a tour that included the Carter Family and the Tennessee Trumpets among it supporting cast. He was promoting the album *Silver*—a particular favorite recorded with Emmylou Harris' producer husband Brian Ahern, whose title celebrated "25 years in the profession." A roster of

BELOW: Johnny Cash joined longtime friend Billy Graham for the closing of the Florida West Coast Crusade in March 1979.

OPPOSITE: Johnny Cash performing at "Explo 72" with June Carter and her family. The Explo 1972 was an evangelical conference and festival that took place in Dallas, Texas, from June 12 to June 17. The event was sponsored by the Campus Crusade for Christ and organized by Paul Eshleman. A crowd of 80,000 mostly young people from over 75 countries congregated to praise Jesus. An even larger crowd of 180,000 came to the nine-hour rock festival that closed the festivities. See pages 110–111.

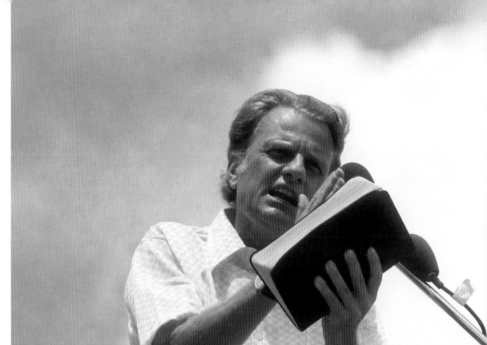

OPPOSITE AND ABOVE: Scenes from Explo '72.

TOP: Billy Graham talked six times at the event, including the finale, the so-called "Christian Woodstock" on June 17, 1972, at which Johnny Cash and Kris Kristofferson played.

BELOW: Johnny, June, and their son John. Johnny's daughter Rosanne stands behind him and June's daughter Carlene is at far right.

BELOW RIGHT: Johnny Cash donned black academic robes to receive an honorary Doctorate of Humane Letters from San Diego's National University on May 8, 1976.

OPPOSITE: Johnny and June perform at the A.P. Carter Memorial Festival in August 1977. Cash frequently performed at the rustic Carter Fold music venue near the Carter Family homeplace at Maces Springs, in rural Southwest Virginia.

guests included the Carter Family and pianist Earl Poole Ball on "(Ghost) Riders in the Sky"); fellow country legend George Jones ("I'll Say It's True"); and Ricky Skaggs and new son-in-law Rodney Crowell, who married Rosanne Cash that year ("Bull Rider").

Also out in 1979 was a gospel double album *A Believer Sings The Truth*. Cash then worked with Jack Clement and Earl Poole Ball on *Rockabilly Blues*, a nod to his ever-popular early days and style. This contained a single, "Without Love," written and produced in London by another new son-in-law, Nick Lowe, who had just

married Carlene Carter. The record featured Lowe and Dave Edmunds, a Carl Perkins-influenced guitarist who played in Lowe's band Rockpile.

In 1980, Johnny Cash was inducted into the Country Music Hall of Fame in Nashville. He became the youngest performer to be given that honor, and was the Hall's youngest living inductee at age forty-eight, but to some it was a signal that his career as a front-line artist was over. Not that Cash saw it that way. He described the accolade as "the greatest public honor I received…nothing beats the Country Music Hall of Fame, or ever will."

At the time of his induction, he had just issued his *Rockabilly Blues* album and was in the middle of recording *The Baron*, released the following March (1981). He would later admit that sometimes in the early part of the decade "I really cared about recording, but sometimes I didn't…I wasn't really motivated and neither was [my record company]."

Marshall Grant had not only played bass from the beginning, but also served as road manager for a quarter-century, keeping Cash safe during his wild, pill-popping years. He left Cash's employ under a cloud in 1980, lawsuits over wrongful termination and alleged embezzlement of retirement funds being settled out of court. Grant went on to manage The Statler Brothers, and Cash recounted in his second autobiography, *Cash*,

that he regretted firing him by letter. "I said things that should have been left unsaid, and I think I made a bad situation worse… it's one of those things in my life that I look back on with a shudder."

The pair remained friends through all of that, and Grant documented his experience with Cash in a 2006 autobiography, *I Was There When It Happened: My Life With Johnny Cash*. The following year saw the Tennessee Two became an inaugural inductee of the Musicians Hall of Fame in 2007, surviving member Grant accompanying John Carter Cash on bass at the ceremony.

The month of April 1981 found Cash in familiar company when two fellow Sun Records survivors joined him on stage in Stuttgart, Germany. Carl Perkins and Jerry Lee Lewis were in the country to play at different events but made time in their schedule to join Johnny at a festival. Fortunately the tapes were rolling and their performance would be released under the appropriate title of *The Survivors*.

This period was undoubtedly the lowest period of Johnny Cash's recording career in terms of his status among record-buyers. His roll-call of albums, once steady sellers or better, went by unremarked and *The Adventures Of Johnny Cash* (1982), *Johnny 99* (1983) and *Rainbow* (1984) failed to catch the public imagination. The second of these contained two songs by Columbia labelmate Bruce Springsteen, the title track and *Highway Patrolman*, but whether these were Cash's choice, that of producer Brian Ahern or his record company is uncertain. He was chopping and changing producers now; Jack Clement and Chips Moman came and went.

Typically, while Johnny's contemporary output was making little impression, repackagings of the past still attracted the critical praise. *Johnny Cash: The Sun Years* was a five-disc set that took advantage of the new digital Compact Disc format to present Cash's 1950s' output to a new generation. Given that rockabilly was enjoying a European revival and that new bands like the Clash were tipping their stylistic hat to the stars and sounds of the 1950s, it was little wonder this material found a new audience. Yet it must have been frustrating to Cash when Columbia Records, his label since 1960, declined to release a new album called *Out Among The Stars*.

He hung onto the master tapes, and the recordings came to light when son John Carter Cash found them gathering dust while he was cataloging his father's private archive in 2012. They were among hundreds of reels of unreleased live and studio recordings in the vault, including the previously mentioned duets with Bob Dylan.

Out Among The Stars, recorded in sessions between 1981 and 1984 with producer Billy Sherrill and featuring duets with June and his old friend Waylon Jennings, was belatedly released in March 2014. John Carter hand-picked the track "She Used To Love Me A Lot," a ballad featuring the plaintive mandolin of a young Marty Stuart, to release ahead of the album. "I really love this song," John Carter Cash told *Rolling Stone* magazine. "The depth that's there reminds me of the real serious stuff that Dad did later in his life. And I truly think it's one of the beautiful undiscovered gems in my father's catalog."

Marty Stuart, a valued member of Cash's backing band at the time of recording, has been quoted as saying that he was "in the very prime of his voice for his lifetime" and that Cash sounds "pitch perfect" on the recordings.

OPPOSITE: Johnny, June, and son John in Copenhagen, 1979.

ABOVE: Cash's stepdaughter Carlene, pictured in 1978 just before her marriage to British producer Nick Lowe, enjoyed brief fame in the early 1990s.

Rockabilly

mechanics, and began performing in nearby churches and schools.

Black outfits fit the group's tight budget. "Nobody had a nice suit then," Johnny explained, "and the only colored shirts we had alike were black."

"Hey Po...
Cry." It ...
copies.

Johnny ...
Luther's ...
boom" gu...
Marshall'...
helped to ...
rockabilly ...
sweeping ...

There's been nothing like rockabilly before or since.

It's an Original form of Music,

And for me it takes me back to basics.

Rockabilly, 1958.

Johnny and the Tennessee Two, 1955. Left to right: Luther Perkins, Johnny, Marshall Grant.

I'm a country boy and a country singer.

But I've always felt that a lot of Count...

... to everybody.

A handbill from one of Johnny's
... 1955.

By early 1957, Johnny had scored major hits with "Folsom Prison Blues" and "I Walk the Line," filled regular engagements on the Louisiana Hayride and the Grand Ole Opry, appeared on network television, and played show dates across much of the South and Midwest.

Johnny signs autographs after one of his early personal appearances.

Johnny's first Sun album, 1957.

This early poster is one of Johnny's keepsakes.

Right, Ernest Tubb welcomes Johnny to the Opry, 1956. Below, a telegram expressing Tubb's goodwill.

Stuart, who went on to become a star in his own right, was at one point married to Cash's daughter Cindy. Johnny had recruited him after he was spotted playing mandolin in Earl Scruggs' band, which he'd joined at the tender age of thirteen. The former teen prodigy added another dimension to Cash's music and, after leaving his employ, would occasionally return—as in the case of 1996's *Unchained* album when he provided a link between Cash and backing band Tom Petty's Heartbreakers (whose bassist Howie Epstein was the live-in lover of stepdaughter Carlene Carter).

Low record sales in the early 1980s meant relative financial hardship, and the Cashes were forced to sell jewelry so that they could pay their domestic staff. And, as John Carter Cash's book *Anchored In Love*, a biography of his mother published after her death, later revealed, tensions in the household ran high at this point.

In one incident, a ten-year-old John witnessed his parents fighting for hours and hours at their second home in Jamaica. While the fights never got physical, June at one point threatened to leave Cash for good, planning to travel to London to stay with her daughter Carlene.

John braced himself to hear bad news when he was eventually summoned to their presence. He was not prepared for the announcement that they had decided to renew their marriage vows.

Cash's difficult increasing dependency on drugs from the late 1950s to late 1960s has already been documented. But a near-deadly cocktail of amphetamines, sleeping pills, and prescription painkillers combined to make his life difficult in the 1980s before a staged intervention took him off to rehab.

LEFT: Cash's music and memory is honored in the Country Music Hall of Fame in Nashville by this visual display.

TOP: Carl Perkins, Johnny Cash, and Jerry Lee Lewis backstage at the Madison Coliseum, Madison, Wisconsin in 1982.

ABOVE: As with his sisters, John Carter Cash was soon playing a part in his parents' stage act.

OPPOSITE: Band member, sometime son-in-law and friend, Marty Stuart.

The physical cause of his problem had been internal bleeding after he had been attacked by—of all things—an ostrich from an exotic animals park he'd established at the House Of Cash. His duodenum, spleen, and part of his stomach were removed in an operation, but this required him to be given another drug: morphine.

His hallucinations and delusions caused his family to have him admitted to the Betty Ford Clinic, where he spent three weeks cleaning up and putting his life on a more even footing.

When in 1985 guitarist Bob Wootton pulled out of shows in Toronto due to a family emergency, Cash called his friend Waylon Jennings to ask if he could find him a replacement. Jennings told him, " 'I play guitar pretty good myself, and I'll come up if you'll let me,' so I didn't call any guitar players. I just went myself—and had more fun than I've had in ten years."

Cash asked Waylon to stand back out of the spotlight until the first few songs had been played. He gradually moved forward until his trademark leather-tooled Telecaster was visible, then "the greatest guitar player in the world" (as Cash introduced him) joined Johnny for a couple of duets.

In the middle of the decade, Cash joined forces with Jennings plus fellow free spirits Willie Nelson and Kris Kristofferson to form a country supergroup called The Highwaymen. Their title came from an evocative song by "Macarthur Park" writer Jimmy Webb, who had recorded it himself in the previous decade, but the lyrical sentiments certainly fitted. (Of the group's four members, Cash was the only one who was not a Texan.)

The quartet's self-titled debut album went to #1 on the country charts and made the pop Top 100. It inspired a follow-up four years later, and its title track bagged a Grammy in February 1986 for Best Country Song. The previous month's American Music Awards at Los Angeles'

Shrine Auditorium had seen the group win two awards in the video category—a new experience for Cash and pals. He would make good use of the new medium in the last part of his career, but it was an early pointer to how powerful a marketing tool the likes of Country Music Television would turn out to be.

Cash's recording contract was due to end in 1986, and it was no surprise when Columbia declined to renew it. Cash had recorded a parody single, "Chicken In Black," about his brain being transplanted into a chicken that he later termed "intentionally atrocious." But, while it reflected his frustrated frame of mind, he believes it was a barrier to finding another label willing to take a chance on an artist "who'd make a mockery of himself." Ironically, the song turned out to be more of a commercial success than any of his other recent material.

Johnny was convinced he could earn a new record contract, but he was not sitting around waiting for one to fall into his lap. He went to play for Jimmy Bowen, the hot production name in Nashville at that point, but claims never to have heard back from him after taking a guitar to his office and attempting to impress him with thirty minutes of music. In 1986, Cash returned to Sun Studios in Memphis to team up with Roy Orbison, Jerry Lee Lewis, and Carl Perkins to create the album *Class Of '55*.

With time on his hands, Cash published his only novel, *Man In White*, a fictional account of the life of Paul the Apostle, written over a period of several years. Billy Graham himself encouraged Cash to finish this book when Cash had started it and then put it aside. He didn't think himself worthy to write about Paul and struggled with the conversion scene until he too had a dream about a vision on a road. The result was described by one internet critic as "totally believable and spiritually uplifting…recommended to Christians and non-Christians alike."

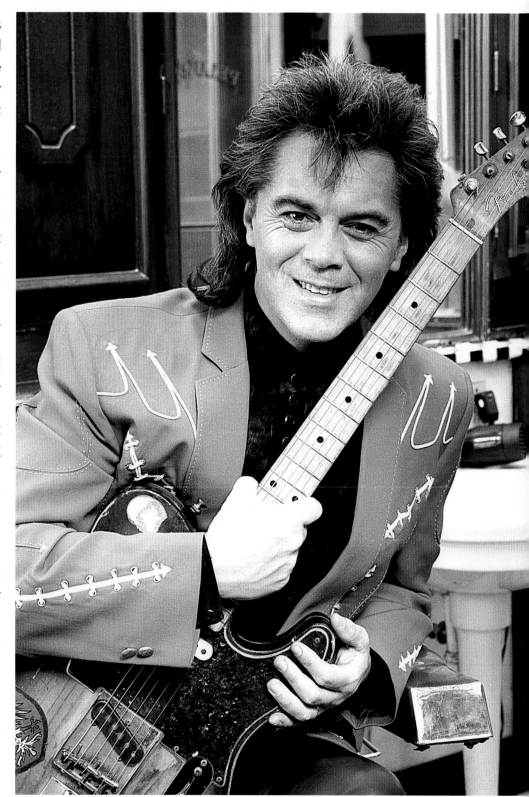

Johnny Cash clearly identified with his protagonist. In an interview, Cash called St. Paul a survivor and an inspiration "who had every kind of reason to quit and never did because of his faith in God." When asked in the same interview if he'd considered changing his attire to "white for redemption," the singer replied, "That would look a little presumptuous."

The year of 1987 brought hope on the recording front as Johnny signed with Mercury Records. He was encouraged to link once more with producer Jack Clement, and all seemed rosy—but a change of personnel at the top not long after left Cash "again an artist the company wasn't interested in promoting."

His short stint with Mercury lasted from 1987 to 1991, his first album in May bearing the optimistic title *Johnny Cash Is Back In Town*. One of the tracks, "The Night Hank Williams Came To Town," would become a live favorite in future years, but the album did battle with *1958–1986: The CBS Years*, one of many hits collections Columbia would bring to the market in the coming years.

1988 was fairly uneventful until its final month, when Cash was admitted to a Nashville hospital for open-heart surgery. He'd called in for a check-up only to be told he had a ninety per cent blockage of two coronary arteries and needed an immediate bypass.

Ever rebellious, he smoked a cigarette half an hour before the two-hour operation, which was a success. Eerily, hellraising Outlaw pal Waylon Jennings had just recovered from a similar operation, while another good friend, Roy Orbison, had died of a heart attack earlier that month; it seemed impossible to discount the trio's shared lifestyle as having contributed to their problems. Happily Waylon, the youngest at 51, survived, as did Cash, the oldest at 56 (the unlucky Orbison was 52).

On emerging from hospital in early January, Cash vowed to exercise and cut out eating fatty foods after what he called "a soul-searching experience." He

OPPOSITE: Cash recording in Memphis, Tennessee. September 1985.

ABOVE: Close friend, fellow member of The Highwaymen, and legendary hell-raiser Waylon Jennings in 1988.

ABOVE: Highwaymen Johnny Cash and Kris Kristofferson on stage in 1985. Kristofferson said later "I loved it, but I just wish now that I'd realised how short it was going to be... I got to stand next to Johnny Cash and sing harmony every night. Now Willie and I are the only ones left. I wish I'd appreciated it more."

OPPOSITE, ABOVE: Johnny Cash recording in Memphis, Tennessee, September 1985.

OPPOSITE BELOW: Waylon Jennings performing with Johnny Cash in the 1970s.

123

retreated to his house in Jamaica, Cinnamon Hill, where he recuperated away from the pressures of the world. The house had been built in 1747 by an ancestor of the poet Elizabeth Barrett Browning and he bought it in the 1970s from a friend, John Rollins. Cash romantically copied out the Browning poem "How Do I Love Thee" and gave it to wife June to mark their property acquisition.

Though the family had been held up at gunpoint by robbers in the house on Christmas Day 1982 it had not affected Cash's affection for the building, its location, and its history. And, at this time, it was certainly the right place for him to make the speediest recovery possible.

In 1988, Cash publicly campaigned for Al Gore as he sought the Democratic presidential nomination. Gore ran his campaign as "a Southern centrist (who) opposed federal funding for abortion. He favored a moment of silence for prayer in the schools and voted against banning the interstate sale of handguns." He lost to Michael Dukakis, but would later serve as vice president under Bill Clinton.

The musical event of the year had occurred in December. *Water From The Wells Of Home*, the seventy-fifth original album in the Cash catalog, was an all-star effort featuring June, John Carter Cash, and guests Paul McCartney, Waylon Jennings, Hank Williams Jr, Glen Campbell, and Emmylou Harris.

The duet with McCartney, "New Moon Over Jamaica," was a clear highlight, while others included JJ Cale's "Call Me The Breeze" and a remake of Cash's own Sun-era "Ballad of A Teenage Queen." This was one of two singles, the other "That Old Wheel," which reached #45 and #21 respectively, but their parent did not fare well on the country album chart, peaking at #48.

Mercury was certainly not rising, and the situation with his record company was not set to improve. "Jack (Clement) and I made some music to be proud of," he recalled in his autobiography, "but it was like singing to an empty hall." He vowed to end his recording career right there and then, contenting himself with playing "with my friends and family to people who really wanted to hear us."

Cash's critical and commercial stock might well have been at a low ebb, but there were still those to whom he was an influence and an inspiration. Proof came in the unlikely shape of *'Til Things Are Brighter: A Tribute To Johnny Cash*, recorded by a roll-call of British musicians like Marc Riley of the Fall and Jon Langford of the Mekons (the executive producers), Pete Shelley of the Buzzcocks, Mary Mary of Gaye Bykers on Acid, and Marc Almond of Soft Cell. As one critic retrospectively remarked, "It's kinda cool that the post-punk generation paid this tribute to someone who, by then, probably was the most anti-cool musician you could cover."

Further interest from the contemporary music scene came when U2 sought him out. The Irish group's Bono and Adam Clayton were on a road trip across America and, after an initial meeting in Hendersonville in 1988, an informal jam session took place. This second meeting in May 1989 set the scene for collaboration in the 1990s. U2 had paid homage to Sun in their "Rattle And Hum" tour and album, recording at the label's studios and using the microphone Elvis had once sung at.

Johnny himself commenced the new decade with *Boom Chicka Boom* an album taking its title from the Tennessee Three's patented sound. Highlights included "Hidden Shame," a song specially written for him by Nick Lowe's friend (and noted country fan) Elvis Costello, and a cover of Harry Chapin's "Cat's In The Cradle." "Don't Go Near The Water," an environmental song originally recorded for 1974's *Ragged Old Flag* album, was revisited, while Cash's mother Carrie made a cameo appearance on "Family Bible." In similarly biblical vein, he also recorded *Johnny Cash Reads The Complete New Testament* in 1990.

Johnny Cash on stage with June, 1987.

The Songwriters Guild of America chose Cash as the 1989 recipient of their highest honor, the Aggie Award, while in 1990 the National Academy of Recording Arts & Sciences (NARAS) acknowledged him as a "Living Legend." This was a big deal, since the category had only been created the previous year when the first Legend Awards were issued to Andrew Lloyd Webber, Liza Minnelli, Smokey Robinson, and Willie Nelson.

The following year saw four more musicians (Aretha Franklin, Billy Joel, and Quincy Jones the others) acknowledged for their "ongoing contributions and influence in the recording field." Legend Awards since 1993 have been sporadic, and fourteen solo musicians

and one band (the Bee Gees) have received it at the time of writing.

It had not been a vintage decade for Johnny Cash, but despite economic stringency in the household he was far from being on his uppers: he had his main home on Old Hickory Lake just outside Nashville, a farm at Bon Aqua, also outside Nashville, a house in Port Richey, Florida, that June had inherited from her parents and his previously mentioned holiday home in Jamaica. Yet with country music pitching to a new, young, affluent audience, and the arrival of digital audio in the shape of the all-conquering compact disc, he seemed more of a musical anachronism than ever.

OPPOSITE: Cash in December 1990 posing with his son John Carter Cash (back left), his wife June, his daughter Rosanne, and her husband Rodney Crowell, after receiving the Grammy Legend Award. At the age of forty-eight Cash became the youngest living inductee into the Country Music Hall of Fame.

ABOVE: New-wave artists Nick Lowe (first left) and Elvis Costello (second left) join in the fun at London's Royal Albert Hall, 1989. Lowe was married to Carlene Carter between 1979 and 1990.

THE JOHNNY CASH SHOW

Between June 7, 1969 and March 31, 1971, ABC TV viewers enjoyed fifty-eight episodes of *The Johnny Cash Show*, filmed at the Ryman Auditorium in Nashville, Tennessee. then home of the Grand Ole Opry. Relatively successful (the show reached #17 in the Nielsen ratings in 1970) it allowed Johnny Cash to bring a host of little-known country artists to the attention of a mainstream audience. There were big names too, of course: Bob Dylan (right) and Joni Mitchell appeared on the first show; later there were appearances by Linda Ronstadt, Kris Kristofferson, Mickey Newbury, Neil Young, Gordon Lightfoot, Merle Haggard, James Taylor, Tammy Wynette, Derek and the Dominos, Creedence Clearwater Revival and also jazz great Louis Armstrong, Stevie Wonder, and Ray Charles.

The show was revived briefly in 1976, on CBS—*Johnny Cash and Friends*—for four weeks from August 29 to September 20, 1976, from the Grand Old Opry in Nashville.

OPPOSITE: *The Johnny Cash Show* introduced many Americans to Country music.

RIGHT: Bob Dylan guested on the first show, on June 7, 1969.

OPPOSITE: The May 1, 1969, shoot for the show saw Johnny and June at home in the Lake House at at 200 Claudill Drive in Hendersonville, TN.

ABOVE: Sold to singer Barry Gibbs and his wife, the house burnt to the ground during remodeling in 2007.

RIGHT: Fire chief Gary Parker (R) talks with Johnny's youngest brother Tommy while they look over the remains of Lake House. Tommy was the realtor who sold Lake House after Johnny's death.

LEFT: On January 20, 1971, *The Johnny Cash Show* was devoted to "The Country Music Story." It collected together a wealth of stars and aired on January 28. Here, Cash and Carl Perkins (1932–1998), "The King of Rockabilly."

BELOW: Eddie Arnold (1918–2008) had 147 songs chart on the *Billboard* Country charts, of which 92 were Top 10 hits and 29 reached #1. The "Pioneer of the Nashville Sound"—also known as the "Tennessee Plowboy"—was one of the volunteers who found the wreckage of Jim Reeves' plane on August 2, 1964, two days after it crashed. He played on *The Johnny Cash Show* aired on January 28, 1971.

OPPOSITE: Tammy Wynette (1942–1998) also appeared on the "The Country Music Story" show and the version of "Stand by Your Man" she sang that day appeared on *The Johnny Cash Show*'s "Best of" CD.

Eric Clapton's Derek and the Dominoes featured in the second series, episode 14 originally aired on January 6, 1971.

LEFT AND OPPOSITE: Cash did two special Christmas shows in 1976 and 1977: the 1976 show appeared on CBS on December 6, 1976. Among the guests were Tony Orlando (left) and Roy Clark. Orlando was at the top of the tree in 1976 having had a huge hit with "Tie a Yellow Ribbon Round the Ole Oak Tree" in 1973 and enjoyed a successful show on CBS 1974–1976, *The Tony Orlando and Dawn Show*. Roy Clark was host of the prestigious *Hee Haw* 1969–1992 and guest-hosted Johnny Carson's *The Tonight Show* in the 1970s.

BELOW: CBS revived *The Johnny Cash Show* between August 29 and September 20, 1976, as *Johnny Cash and Friends*. Here, Kris Kristofferson duets with Cash on September 15, 1976. They would go on to play together in The Highwaymen from 1985.

6

REJUVENATION 1990–1997

"You've got a song you're singing from your gut, you want that audience to feel it in their gut. And you've got to make them think that you're one of them sitting out there with them too. They've got to be able to relate to what you're doing."

Johnny Cash

The 1990s had started unpromisingly, with both Cash and son undergoing spells in rehab. Johnny had managed to stay off drugs for several years, but in 1989 entered Nashville's Cumberland Heights Alcohol and Drug Treatment Center. Three years later he entered the Loma Linda Behavioral Medicine Center in Loma Linda, California for his final rehab, John Carter Cash following him several months later.

Things had gone from bad to worse when, in March 1991, Cash lost his beloved mother Carrie. She was eighty-six and had just undergone treatment for cancer. It was an understandable blow to him, and he shed public tears for the woman whose guidance had kept him on the straight and narrow, encouraging his musical leanings and reminding him about his duties to God. For the last ten years of her life, Carrie Cash had served at the gift shop she had encouraged Johnny to set up at the House Of Cash studio/museum complex.

Unfortunately, and also close to home, the early 1990s saw June waging her own battle with prescription drugs. She stopped speaking in full sentences and would drift off into her own world. "She maintained strong control of her addiction," son John later said, adding that any attempts at confrontation were pointless. Johnny, still troubled by his own demons, was reluctant to step in.

In 1992 Cash was inducted into the Rock and Roll Hall of Fame, becoming one of only a handful of artists to grace both the rock and country halls. Lyle Lovett, one of many

singers to have explicitly acknowledged his influence, was the man doing the honors. Other performers to be inducted along with Cash included Bobby Blue Bland, Booker T and the MGs, late guitarists Elmore James and Jimi Hendrix, guitarmaker Leo Fender, and the Isley Brothers.

" 'I Walk The Line' was the first song of his I ever heard," said Lovett in his speech, continuing by stating that his aunt had owned the Cash single and he and his cousin would play it at loud volume when she went out. "He helped show the world what happens when rural sensibilities and values mix with the urban environment. He has never been afraid to record songs with social commentary and has been eager to seek out new songs by young songwriters like Bob Dylan, Kris Kristofferson, and Bruce Springsteen.

"He's had forty-eight songs on the pop charts, 135 on the country charts, and he's sold more than fifty million records. His music his artistry and his point of view helped form and define what we know as rock'n'roll," summed up an awestruck Lovett, adding: "This is the biggest deal of my life!"

Cash walked on to a standing ovation and, after embracing Lovett, started by thanking Sam Phillips and Jack Clement. He recalled his early days buying records by his heroes, Hank Williams and Hank Snow, the Carter Family and others. "I listened to WHBQ and they had a program called Red Hot And Blue which late at night would play what they called race music. There I heard some of my

OPPOSITE: Cash faced the 1990s with a determination to justify his status as one of American music's acknowledged greats and sell records again.

A new decade—Johnny and June off stage in 1991 (LEFT) and Cash doing what he did best (RIGHT).

Robert Duvall and Johnny Cash after the twenty-sixth Annual Academy of Country Music Awards at Universal Amphitheater in Universal City, CA, 1991.

earliest heroes…Sister Rosetta Tharpe, singing those great gospel songs. I bought field recordings by Alan Lomax…they influenced a lot of my writing, songs like 'Big River' and 'Get Rhythm'. Pink Anderson, Blind Lemon Jefferson."

"Whether I belong here or not I'm extremely proud," he said, namechecking June, Carlene, and Rosanne, as well as John Carter Cash. He finished by saying he'd had a chat with Little Richard before they went on and decided "God was watching over tonight."

Johnny Cash was a living legend, of that there was no doubt—but even legends have to pay the rent and he was playing remarkably small venues. Only with his famous friends could he play the larger halls, so it was a relief when The Highwaymen saddled up again. A second album, *Highwayman 2*, had been released in 1990. It again breached the pop Top 100 in the United States, making #2 in the country chart. There was clearly an audience for the quartet, as was proven with tours of the U.S. and Australasia. A six-date British tour filled arenas in April 1992, with fans flocking to see Waylon, Willie, Kris, and Cash join forces.

A few months prior to this had seen Johnny place a note in the old Western Wall of Jerusalem (not for the first time—see photo page 99); superstition suggests God reads such missives left in its cracks. It was clear Cash still felt he had messages to impart, and he appeared alongside his fellow Highwaymen once again that summer to lend his weight to a Back to the Ranch Nature Benefit festival in Montauk on Long Island at the invitation of Paul Simon.

October saw Bob Dylan's thirtieth anniversary as a recording artist celebrated by the great and the good at New York's Madison Square Garden. June and Johnny had sung on "It Ain't Me Babe," their duet hit from the late 1960s, and one audience member in particular, metal/rap producer Rick Rubin, was impressed by the reaction of the younger members of the audience to this veteran sixty-two-year-old performer. The seeds of an idea were sown in his head, and it would not be long before they started to flower.

Meanwhile, Johnny was considering following in the footsteps of Glen Campbell and starting his own venue where he could play seventy-five theater shows a year without the problem of having to tour. Cash Country was to be situated in Branson, Missouri (where Campbell's

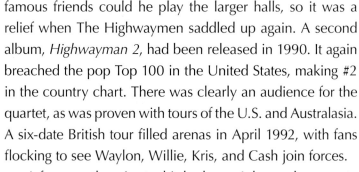

LEFT: Cash performs at a Billy Graham rally in Central Park, New York, September 22, 1991.

OPPOSITE: Cash with (L–R) June, Rosanne, Carlene, and son John at the seventh annual Rock and Roll Hall of Fame induction ceremony, New York, New York, January 15, 1992.

Goodtime Theatre was situated), and would be nothing less than a $35 million music theme park. Unfortunately the venture foundered, and the singer was fortunate to have lent only his name to the venture rather than his money.

The contact made with U2 in the late 1980s finally bore musical fruit when, in 1993, he was playing a gig in Dublin with Kris Kristofferson. He used the event to link up with the quartet in the studio and record a track, "The Wanderer," that would appear on the Irish group's *Zooropa* album. Singer Bono wrote the biblical-inspired track with Cash in mind, and when the album was released the following year it sold seven million copies. Suddenly, as had happened several times before, a new audience was being alerted to Johnny Cash.

Country music was going through a period of rejuvenation, with younger "alt.country" acts taking the place of older, tired talents. This might not have worked to Johnny Cash's advantage, but he was revered by these newcomers and was not seen as one of the "old guard." The late-1980s British tribute album turned out to be the first leaf in the growing wind, and the likes of Whiskeytown's Ryan Adams would soon be performing Cash songs in concert.

Cash flew home from Dublin and, at a gig in Santa Ana California two weeks later, was introduced to Rick Rubin, the man who'd seen him at the Dylan concert and been entranced. Rubin ran the Def American record label—and, while Cash had never heard of the edgy artists that

LEFT: Johnny jams with Keith Richards, one of his biggest fans, after the 1992 Rock and Roll Hall of Fame inauguration. Keith was influenced by Luther Perkins, and said how much he loved Cash's cover of Hank Williams' "I Heard That Lonesome Whistle Blow."

RIGHT: Johnny Cash in 1994.

"They [Cash and Perkins] taught me about the importance of silence in music— that you don't have to play all over the song."

Keith Richard

ABOVE: Cash, Ron Wood, George Harrison, and Roger McGuinn help Bob Dylan celebrate his thirty years as a recording artist, New York, 1992.

RIGHT: The Highwaymen—from left, Willie Nelson, Waylon Jennings (center, arms out), Kris Kristofferson (second right, rear), and Johnny Cash (right)—perform at Central Park Summer-Stage, New York, May 23, 1993. The month before they had performed for Farm Aid at Ames, Iowa.

comprised its roster, his outlaw image fascinated Rubin enough to make him an offer.

The result was a series of Rubin-produced albums called, simply, "American Recordings" (as the Def American label was renamed, Cash's album was the first release under the new branding). It was a partnership that would prove as fruitful in his later years as had that with Don Law in the late 1950s. "When I first started recording with Rick, word got out that I was 'happening,' whatever that meant. But I really felt it was—like something really was happening. It felt really good to know that there was a possibility that I had an audience among the young people out there."

The first *American Recordings* album resulted from six months of work in Rick Rubin's home and various Californian recording studios. Cash clocked up nearly 100 songs in that period, ranging widely in style and origin.

At the end of recording, Rubin persuaded him to do some solo shows at Johnny Depp's Viper Rooms to road test the concept in front of an audience. It was the first time ever Cash had appeared "naked" without backing musicians, with just an acoustic guitar for company, but the buzz his triumphant performance created with sold-out, celebrity -

packed audiences reverberated through the media. Johnny Cash was back…and in better form than ever!

"When I got with Rick and things started happening," he told journalist Sylvie Simmons, "It felt so good to be back holding the reins myself and doing something people appreciated." Rubin, he said, reminded him of Sam Phillips in his early recording years. "It was that same kind of freedom— Sam and Rick both put me in front of that microphone and said, 'Let's hear what you've got, sing your heart out,' and I'd sing one or two and they'd say, 'Sing another one, let's hear more.' And I just kept right on singing."

His first *American Recordings* album appeared in April 1994 and contained two songs cut live at the Viper Room, "Tennessee Stud" and "The Man Who Couldn't Cry" in its thirteen tracks. "The Beast In Me" was written and originally recorded by Nick Lowe; Leonard Cohen, Tom Waits, and Loudon Wainwright were among the other writers, while the track "Thirteen" was specially penned by Glenn Danzig.

The album was a groundbreaker in so many ways, from the striking cover photo taken in Australia through the video for first single "Delia's Gone" (directed by U2 associate Anton Corbijn), and it was no surprise when *American*

OPPOSITE: Country boy Cash takes time out with rod and line in the 1990s.

BELOW: Two icons of American music, Johnny Cash and soul star Al Green, meet in 1995.

Recordings was declared Best Contemporary Folk Album at the following year's Grammy Awards.

Cash was delighted but far from overwhelmed. "According to the media at the time, that caused an overnight change in my status from 'Nashville has-been' to 'hip icon.' Whatever they called me, I was grateful. It was my second major comeback; the minor ones have been too many to count."

Cash rated this "a very special Grammy (that) proved a lot of things to a lot of people—to Mercury/Polygram, to CBS, to everybody else at the record companies."

That summer, Cash was invited to play at Britain's most prestigious open-air event, the Glastonbury Festival in

OPPOSITE: Cash performs on stage at Glastonbury Festival, June 1994. Promoter Michael Eavis rated him his best ever booking, and Cash gained a new young UK audience. The sixteen-song set started with "Folsom Prison Blues" and "Get Rythm," included "Ring of Fire," "(Ghost) Riders in the Sky," "Big River," and "Jackson" as well as a cover of Leonard Cohen's "Bird on a Wire," and finished with "A Boy Named Sue."

ABOVE: The Highwaymen play *The Tonight Show With Jay Leno* in May 1995, the year the country supergroup released its third and final album.

Somerset. Organiser Michael Eavis went out on a limb, but later declared it one of his best ever bookings.

"He was spellbinding, bloody brilliant," Eavis later said. "That was one of my best bookings of all time. This was when Johnny wasn't nearly as fashionable as he was after 'Hurt.' Some of the youngsters thought I'd gone crazy, as they believed I should be booking new stuff all the time. They thought he was just a daft old country singer. But he was so good. I can't choose one song as my favourite, I'd have a shortlist of 100."

The Highwaymen reconvened yet again for *The Road Goes On Forever*, a 1995 release titled by a Robert Earl Keen song. This would prove The Highwaymen's last album prior to Jennings' death in 2002; its recording was documented a short documentary entitled *Live Forever—In The Studio With The Highwaymen.*

The second Rubin-produced American Recordings album, *Unchained*, was released in 1996, two years on from its predecessor. Its recording had been hampered by a jaw injury Cash suffered that would require multiple operations, yet the result was rated #5 in *Rolling Stone* magazine's prestigious Album of the Year list. *Unchained* received a Grammy for Best Country Album and Cash was nominated for Best Male Country Vocal Performance for his version of "Rusty Cage."

In contrast to the stark solo nature of its predecessor, backing had been supplied by Tom Petty and the Heartbreakers with guest appearance by Red Hot Chili Peppers bassist Flea on "Spiritual" and Lindsey Buckingham and Mick Fleetwood, both of Fleetwood Mac, on "Sea Of Heartbreak." The result was more country-rock than folk, while only three songs were Cash originals—two revisiting earlier, Sun-era glories in the shape of "Mean Eyed Cat" and "Country Boy."

In his second autobiography *Cash*, published in 1997, the singer outlined a project that "really has my blood up"—a series of spiritual songs he and Rubin were planning to record in a cathedral. "Rock has scouted out a location that might work. I can't wait," said Cash, who admitted he had "no idea what my long-term recording future will hold."

As events would soon show, it was not just his recording future that was in the balance.

"I love songs about horses, railroads, land, Judgment Day, family, hard times, whiskey, courtship, marriage, adultery, separation, murder, war, prison, rambling, damnation, home, salvation, death, pride, humor, piety, rebellion, patriotism, larceny, determination, tragedy, rowdiness, heartbreak and love. And Mother. And God." Johnny Cash

Cash poses for a picture November 14, 1996, in San Francisco, CA. As an emeritus member of both the Country Music and Rock & Roll Halls of Fame and winner of the 1991 Grammy Legend Award, and with more than a 150 charted hits and over 1,500 songs recorded, Johnny Cash—now the Grand Old Man of Nashville—saw his career revivified.

American Recordings: Unchained

Released: November 5, 1996

Recorded: 1995–1996

Label: American/Warner Bros.

Producer: Rick Rubin

1 "Rowboat" (Beck) – 3:44

2 "Sea of Heartbreak" (Paul Hampton, Hal David) – 2:42

3 "Rusty Cage" (Chris Cornell) – 2:49

4 "The One Rose (That's Left in My Heart)" (Del Lyon/Lani McIntire) – 2:26

5 "Country Boy" (Cash) – 2:31

6 "Memories Are Made of This" (Richard Dehr/Terry Gilkyson/Frank Miller) – 2:19

7 "Spiritual" (Josh Haden) – 5:06

8 "Kneeling Drunkard's Plea" (Maybelle Carter/Anita Carter/Helen Carter/June Carter Cash) – 2:32

9 "Southern Accents" (Tom Petty) – 4:41

10 "Mean Eyed Cat" (Cash) – 2:33

11 "Meet Me in Heaven" (Cash) – 3:21

12 "I Never Picked Cotton" (Bobby George/Charles Williams) – 2:39

13 "Unchained" (Jude Johnstone) – 2:51

14 "I've Been Everywhere" (Geoff Mack) – 3:17

Personnel:

Tom Petty (left and below) Vocals, Acoustic Guitar, Electric Guitar, Bass, Chamberlin

Mike Campbell Acoustic Guitar, Electric Guitar, Bass, Mandolin, Dobro

Benmont Tench Piano, Hammond B3 Organ, Vox Continental Organ, Harmonium, Chamberlin

Howie Epstein Acoustic Guitar, Bass

Steve Ferrone/ Curt Bisquera (on 7,8) Drums & Percussion

Marty Stuart Acoustic Guitar, Electric Guitar, Bass

Flea Bass on 7; Lindsey Buckingham Acoustic Guitar on 2; Mick Fleetwood Percussion on 2; Juliet Prater Percussion on 3

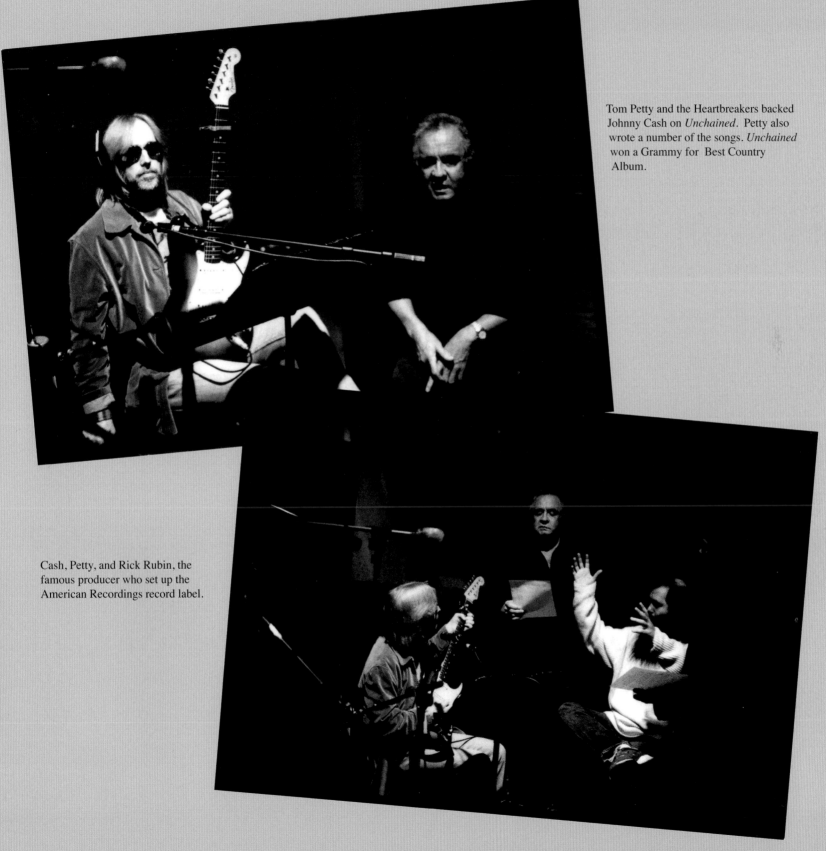

Tom Petty and the Heartbreakers backed
Johnny Cash on *Unchained*. Petty also
wrote a number of the songs. *Unchained*
won a Grammy for Best Country
Album.

Cash, Petty, and Rick Rubin, the
famous producer who set up the
American Recordings record label.

7

FINAL YEARS

"There's no way around grief and loss: you can dodge all you want, but sooner or later you just have to go into it, through it, and, hopefully, come out the other side. The world you find there will never be the same as the world you left."

Johnny Cash in *Cash*

In his eventful lifetime, Johnny Cash had put his music before family, friends, pretty much everything but his God. But time would catch up with him, as it does with everyone. Given the abuse to which he'd subjected himself over the years, it was amazing he was still performing halfway through his seventh decade.

But performing he most certainly was. The year of 1997 found him touring with daughter Cindy. Audiences in Nashville on October 23 observed him to be uncharacteristically sloppy, and their calls for an encore were ignored—an almost unheard-of occurrence.

It was during a show in Flint, Michigan, two days later that Cash first revealed he was seriously ill and fighting a form of Parkinson's Disease. He dropped the bombshell after nearly falling over trying to retrieve a guitar pick, and insisted bravely that "It's all right. I refuse to give it some ground in my life." Cindy "saw the fear in his eyes" and waited for him at the side of the stage as he bade his audience farewell. When she tried to assist him, his entourage surrounded him. "It scared him to be sick," she later said, "and I couldn't get to him…I felt like I was going to hit someone that night."

The initial diagnosis was Shy-Drager Syndrome, a neurodegenerative disease in which cells in the brain or in the spinal chord are lost. The illness has no definitive treatment, and can only be slowed down at best. The end of the year saw the Cash family regroup at their Jamaican holiday home, which would prove even more of a haven for him in his final years than it had in the past.

In 2000, the diagnosis was altered to autonomic neuropathy. As was the case for Cash, the disease often comes as a consequence of diabetes and attacks internal organs such as the bladder and the cardiovascular system as well as weakening the immune system.

The inevitable headlines that followed his dramatic, unscheduled announcement cast an understandable shadow over the final years of Cash's life, even though he managed to make a few live appearances and record two more albums. "I've had forty-three years of touring," he told *Rolling Stone* magazine. "That's enough. I can direct my energies more to recording now. I intend to keep recording as long as I'm able. It's what I do. It's what I feel."

His illness resulted in him being hospitalized in 1998 for severe pneumonia, which damaged his lungs, and it was clear that, as he approached seventy, Johnny Cash's public appearances would now be few and far between. One was in April 1999 at an all-star tribute show to himself starring Bob Dylan, Willie Nelson, Bruce Springsteen, Kris Kristofferson, and many more.

Johnny and June at a concert hosted by the Recording Industry Association of America in Washington D.C. April 16, 1997.

BELOW: Cash pictured at the *TNT All Star Tribute* to himself, recorded and aired on television in April 1999.

OPPOSITE: President George W. and First Lady Laura Bush congratulate Johnny as he receives the National Medal of the Arts in Washington DC, 2002.

One particular live appearance in front of the television cameras before his illness became public knowledge had resulted in *VH1 Storytellers: Johnny Cash & Willie Nelson*, an album recorded in 1997 and released the following June that began with a duet on the old hit "(Ghost) Riders in the Sky" and then saw the two grand old men of American song alternating vocals over fifteen songs. It made #25 in the country chart, #56 pop, *People* magazine somewhat remarkably describing it as "a landmark in pop country music."

In keeping with the show's concept, Cash recounted the stories that inspired his art, while Nelson's biggest insight was that he wrote his three greatest songs ("Funny How Time Slips Away," "Crazy," and "Night Life") in one single week. "If you were hoping for camaraderie and warmth, it's here,' said *No Depression* magazine. "However, if you were hoping this felicitous pairing might produce a brilliant tribute to stand testimony to a portion of the amazing body of work these two artists have produced over a lifetime, this is not that recording."

In 1999, Johnny Cash received a very special Grammy. The Lifetime Achievement Award is awarded by the Recording Academy to "performers who, during their lifetimes, have made creative contributions of outstanding artistic significance to the field of recording." This is distinct from the Grammy Hall of Fame Award, which honors specific recordings rather than individuals, and the Grammy Trustees Award, which honors non-performers. Fellow nominees were the late soul superstars Sam Cooke, Otis Redding, plus living soul legend Smokey Robinson, and smooth jazz singer Mel Tormé.

In 2001 he'd team this with the National Medal of Arts, the country's highest award for artistic excellence, while 1999 also saw June pick up a Grammy of her own for the solo acoustic album *Press On*.

The third album in the American Recordings series, *American III: Solitary Man*, was released in October 2000.

It was Cash's highest charting (#11 country) solo studio LP since 1976's *One Piece at a Time*. A version of Tom Petty's belligerent "I Won't Back Down" appeared to be a response to his illness, while he also covered "One" as a tip of the hat to Irish friends U2.

Cash's two previous albums produced by Rick Rubin had been Grammy winners, and this kept up the run. His version of Neil Diamond's 1966 song "Solitary Man" won the award for Best Male Country Vocal Performance.

Johnny Cash's eighty-seventh and final album of his career was also the fourth in the American Recordings series. Released in November 2002, *American IV: The Man Comes Around* saw Cash return to a sparser, solo style. Most songs were covers, and the theme was mortality with a capital M. Songs like Lennon and McCartney's "In My Life," the traditional "Danny Boy" and The Eagles' doomed gunfighter ballad "Desperado" were delivered (the last-named with the help of its co-writer, Don Henley) in a way that made it clear that this was indeed the Man in Black's final act. The album went platinum, reached #22 in the *Billboard* pop listing and #2 on the country chart. It was also Cash's first non-compilation album to go gold in thirty years, selling over 500,000 copies and progressing to platinum in the wake of his death.

LEFT: Cash pictured with close friend and fellow Highwayman Willie Nelson at the *TNT All Star Tribute* in April 1999.

RIGHT: Author Peggy Knight was companion, confidante, and caretaker to Johnny Cash for thirty-three years. She met Maybelle Carter at a local VFW Hall for Bingo Nite in 1967, and has related events in three books: *My 33 Years in the House of Cash*, *Cooking in the House of Cash*, and *At Home with Johnny, June, and Mother Maybelle*. In September 2005, Peggy Knight was inducted into the Old Time Country Music Hall of Fame in September in recognition of her significant contributions in the "preservation, promotion, and performance of traditional country music locally, nationally, and internationally."

The catalyst for this sales success was the Grammy-winning video for "Hurt," a song written by Trent Reznor of Nine Inch Nails in 1994 and a controversial choice of material for Cash to record. Even his son John Carter Cash, who grew up as a fan of the group, had reservations. Reznor admitted that he was initially "flattered" but worried that "the idea sounded a bit gimmicky." When he heard the song "it was very strange. It was this other person inhabiting my most personal song. Hearing it was like someone kissing your girlfriend. It felt invasive."

Reznor later modified his opinion and deemed it a great honor, saying: "Having Johnny Cash, one of the greatest singer-songwriters of all time, want to cover your song, that's something that matters to me. It's not so much what other people think but the honor that this guy felt it was worthy of interpreting.

"(Cash) said afterwards it was a song that sounds like one he would have written in the 1960s and that's wonderful."

The video was shot by director Mark Romanek at Cash's Tennessee home. Due to his subject's poor health, Romanek, famous for directing videos for contemporary acts like Madonna, Beck, and Audioslave, had heard the song several months before the album was released and fell in love with its stark sound. There followed several attempts to convince Rick Rubin to let him shoot the clip, even offering to do it for free. The result earned six nominations for the 2003 MTV Video Music Awards and won Best Cinematography.

"This [concept] is completely and utterly alien to what videos are supposed to be," Romanek said, revealing that he had only a few days to conceive and shoot the video before Cash left for Jamaica.

"Videos are supposed to be eye candy—hip and cool and all about youth and energy. This one is about someone [moving] toward the twilight of his career, this powerful, legendary figure who is dealing with issues and emotions you're not used to encountering in videos."

Romanek made the clip with no commercial expectations or calculations, fully expecting that it would not be shown on major video outlets.

W.S. Holland, drummer with the Tennessee Three, put into words his feelings, and those of many other bemused long-time fans: "It sounds odd just saying it, but you know Johnny Cash may be remembered someday more for his video than any of his records."

By this time Johnny Cash's deteriorating health was causing much concern both in his family and among his fans. As it happened, June Carter Cash predeceased him by four months, passing away at the Baptist Hospital in

LEFT: Cash pictured in Nashville in 2000, three years before his death.

BELOW: The personal and professional partnership of June Carter and Johnny Cash ended with her death in May 2003, age 73. Cash followed four months afterwards.

Nashville. Her husband and family members were at her bedside.

She had had an operation to replace a valve on May 7 and died eight days later. She was seventy-three. Two thousand people turned up to the funeral lovingly arranged by Cash, who afterwards steeped himself in work to obliterate the pain of his wife's death.

But it soon became obvious he could not go on without June. He refused to sleep in their bed and gave away all the furniture she had bought. He made a couple of surprise performances at her home town in Virginia, fulfilling a promise to June and reading a tribute to his wife before singing "Ring Of Fire." But it made for painful watching: Cash barely made it to the end of the song.

On September 12, 2003, news broke that Johnny Cash had died at the same Baptist Hospital in the early hours of the morning. The cause of death was complications from diabetes, which resulted in respiratory failure. Manager Lou Robin said. "I hope that friends and fans of Johnny will pray for the Cash family to find comfort during this very difficult time."

The news came just days after he was released from a Tennessee hospital, where he had been resident for two weeks while he was treated for an unspecified stomach ailment. His admission to the hospital on August 25 had forced him to miss the MTV Video Music Awards in New York City, where the video for "Hurt" won in the best cinematography category.

At age seventy-one, with all his children and sixteen grandchildren still alive, Cash was interred in Hendersonville Memory Gardens near his home in Hendersonville, Tennessee. June Carter Cash was still by his side.

RIGHT: Kris Kristofferson attends the funeral at the Hendersonville First Baptist Church, September 15, 2003.

OPPOSITE: Pallbearers carry the casket of the late, great Johnny Cash.

OPPOSITE: A black shroud and roses adorn the plaque marking Cash's induction into the Country Music Hall of Fame.

LEFT: Happier times—Johnny, June, and John Carter Cash (age six), during Hollywood Walk of Fame dedication ceremony on March 9, 1976, when Cash became the 1,669th personality to be honored by the Hollywood Chamber of Commerce.

ABOVE: On his death, the star's fans left flowers and mementoes at his star.

8

THE LEGACY

"I feel music has lost one of its great heroes and the country has lost one of its most authentic voices."

Sheryl Crow

Tributes poured in for a man who had been an icon of American country music for nearly half a century and had impacted popular culture on many levels. U2 singer Bono led the tributes, likening Cash to an oak tree in a garden of weeds. "I considered myself a friend, he considered me a fan—he indulged me." Rolling Stone Mick Jagger "loved him as singer and a writer... His influence spread over many generations of different people."

Nick Cave, representing a newer generation, said: "He had such a wealth of experience in his voice, heaven and hell, and no-one could touch him."

Merle Kilgore, best man at Johnny and June Carter's wedding and co-writer of "Ring Of Fire," reported "a sad day in Tennessee, but a great day in Heaven. The Man in Black is now wearing white as he joins his wife June in the angel band."

Former son-in-law and guitarist Marty Stuart admitted he had "lost one of my best friends. It leaves a dark void in my life that is blacker than any coat he ever wore. He is irreplaceable."

Another former son-in-law Rodney Crowell was "deeply saddened by the loss of my children's grandfather and my very dear friend. The citizens of the world have lost one of their most enduring guiding lights. He will stand as a musical hero to millions, a trailblazing artist, humanitarian, spiritual leader, social commentator and most importantly, patriarch to one of the most varied and colorful extended families imaginable."

Even George W Bush weighed in with his own Presidential tribute: "Johnny Cash was a music legend and American icon whose career spanned decades and genres. His resonant voice and human compassion reached the hearts and souls of generations, and he will be missed. Laura joins me in sending our thoughts and prayers to his family."

Cash had certainly reclaimed the limelight prior to his death, thanks largely to the video for "Hurt." A posthumous stream of product, both previously unreleased and otherwise, was almost inevitable. First to surface was *Unearthed*, a box set released two months after his death The first three discs featured outtakes and alternate versions of songs recorded for his four American Recordings albums while a fourth, *My Mother's Hymn Book*, featured gospel songs Cash learned from his mother as a child. A final disc offered a "best of" the first four American albums. This sold well and was certified gold by the RIAA the following year.

On November 10, 2003, the great and the good gathered at Nashville's Ryman Auditorium to celebrate the life of a legend in story and song. *The Johnny Cash Memorial Tribute: A Celebration of Friends And Family* was broadcast on CMT the following weekend. Actor Tim Robbins acted as host.

Daughter Rosanne kicked off the evening with a bittersweet version of "I Still Miss Someone." Surviving Highwaymen Willie Nelson and Kris Kristofferson were joined by George Jones and Hank Williams Jr. "Jackson"

Country artists perform in a tribute to the late Johnny Cash at the 37th Annual CMA Awards at the Grand Ole Opry House November 5, 2003.

was performed by Brooks & Dunn, with Carlene Carter guesting, while other performers ranged from Tennessee Three member Marshall Grant through Rodney Crowell and Marty Stuart to rapper Kid Rock and Randy Scruggs. Video tributes came from, among others, Bono, Billy Graham, and Trent Reznor.

At a party prior to the concert, friend, and politician Al Gore remembered Cash as a good friend and a "great, great man... We had so many talks about things he cared about deeply. He was politically active, he testified before state legislatures on prison reform, and he campaigned for the rights of Native Americans, and he was real progressive," Gore said. "He didn't think the most important thing was to get more money for rich people. He cared about the poor and the downtrodden."

Fans with and without tickets made their own pilgrimage to Nashville from every state for the event. Many circled the Ryman, waving to the artists as they arrived. A public outpouring of emotion such as this was reminiscent of the mourning for Elvis Presley.

The concert concluded with "We'll Meet Again," which Cash had recorded on his final album. Artists from the concert joined the Cash/Carter family on stage after the first verses, the audience singing along in an emotional showing of affection.

The Johnny Cash story moved from the small to the big screen in 2005, in the form of bio-pic *Walk The Line*. Directed by James Mangold, it charted Cash's rise to fame from his early life picking cotton in Arkansas through to the end of the 1960s.

Filmed the previous summer with an estimated budget of $28,000,000, the movie would recoup the investment ten times over at the box office. But getting the movie produced was not all plain sailing. It had taken four years for the producers to secure the rights to the story from James Keach, a friend of Cash's family, and another four years to get the film made by 20th Century

OPPOSITE: Willie Nelson and Sheryl Crow during a tribute concert at the Ryman Auditorium in Nashville, Tennessee, November 10, 2003.

RIGHT: Former U.S. Vice President Al Gore talked about Johnny, during the same tribute concert.

Walk the Line

Released: September 4, 2005 (at the Telluride
    Festival), November 18, 2005 (U.S.)

Distributer: 20th Century-Fox

Director: James Mangold

Producer: Rick Rubin

Awards: 5 Academy Award nominations
    (Witherspoon won Best Actress); 4 BAFTA
    nominations (won Best Actress and Best Sound);
    3 Golden Globes (Best Actor, Best Actress, Best
    Film); many others

Starring:

Joaquin Phoenix	Johnny Cash
Reese Witherspoon	June Carter Cash
Ginnifer Goodwin	Vivian Cash
Robert Patrick	Ray Cash
Shelby Lynne	Carrie Cash
Sandra Ellis Lafferty	Maybelle Carter
Dallas Roberts	Sam Phillips
Dan John Miller	Luther Perkins
Larry Bagby	Marshall Grant
Clay Steakley	W.S. "Fluke" Holland

OPPOSITE: Co-stars Joaquin Phoenix and Reese Witherspoon pose at the news conference for *Walk The Line* at the 30th Toronto International Film Festival.

ABOVE: Crowds at the Beacon Theater, New York City, for the premiere of *Walk The Line* November 18, 2005.

BELOW: Reese Witherspoon poses backstage with her Oscar statuette for Best Actress in a Leading Role for *Walk The Line* during the 78th Annual Academy Awards on March 5, 2006.

OPPOSITE: Bob Wootton performing with the Tennessee Three celebrates the DVD release of *Walk The Line* at a special Arclight screening featuring live musical performances by the movie's cast.

Fox: Sony, Universal, Focus Features, Paramount, Columbia Pictures, and Warner Bros had all previously passed on the project.

Along with the worldwide acclaim came a Best Actress Oscar for Reece Witherspoon, who played June to Joaquin Phoenix' Johnny. The movie and its principals also won Comedy or Musical Golden Globes for Best Performance by an Actor in a Motion Picture, Best Performance by an Actress in a Motion Picture and Best Motion Picture. Witherspoon took a BAFTA for her acting and the movie was in total nominated for seventy awards, winning half that number.

Walk the Line focused primarily on the long courtship of Johnny and June Carter, and flows as an extended flashback from Cash getting ready to take the stage at his historic Folsom Prison Concert in early 1968. One benefit of the movie is that is reminds us not to underestimate how influential Johnny Cash was in his day. He was part of the movement which made country music more acceptable in the United States in the 1960s, as part of a search for an authentic America. One signal of this change was when Bob Dylan recorded his 1969 *Nashville Skyline* album and included a duet with Cash.

While still alive, Johnny had approved Joaquin Phoenix to play him in the movie because he liked his performance in the movie *Gladiator* (2000) in which Phoenix played the cowardly and malicious Emperor Commodus. Cash invited Phoenix to his house for dinner. June Carter Cash also approved Reese Witherspoon for her role before she died.

After visiting many of Cash's old homes, production designer David J. Bomba created ninety sets for the movie to underline the contrast between Cash's two lives, one set in the cotton fields of his youth and the other in the fast-moving world of music. Johnny and June's actual home, in Hendersonville, was a location in the movie.

Walk The Line is a very traditional love story. The number of awards won by Phoenix and Witherspoon show how well they worked their way into the characters and made the movie feel convincing, when it might have seemed shallow and sugary.

Rather than use Cash recordings as the soundtrack to the movie, Phoenix and Witherspoon performed all of the songs themselves, without being dubbed. This meant they had to learn to play their instruments (guitar and autoharp) from scratch and had vocal training for six months with music producer T-Bone Burnett. Some critics felt that the decision to make new versions of Cash's songs rather than have the actors lip-synch over existing recordings was a risky one,

but in the end the results were more than respectable. Cash and Carter don't get to sing in their own voices until the end of the movie, but it demonstrates that the music Cash championed can live on after his lifetime in other voices.

Cash's first wife Vivian Liberto died age seventy-one in 2005, the year *Walk The Line* premiered. Daughter Kathy had been so upset at the portrayal of her mother that she walked out of a private pre-release screening, so perhaps it is merciful that Vivian never saw the movie.

Things might have been more difficult had Rosanne not been instrumental in having some scenes unflattering to her

mother removed. "The movie was painful," she said. "The three of them were not recognizable to me as my parents in any way. But the scenes were recognizable, so the whole thing was fraught with sadness because they all had just died…but I have no impulse to set the record straight."

She added that "My dad and June wanted [the movie] to happen, but it was torture for my mother [Vivian]. The idea that her worst nightmare—she's a strict Catholic girl who had to get divorced—is out there…it was intolerable to her. I thought it was very ironic that she died a few months before it came out."

Rather than retire hurt after divorcing Johnny, Vivian had thrown herself into life and the community. She remarried, to local police officer, Dick Distin, in 1968 and remained in Ventura, a valued member of the community. She was a long-serving president of the Garden Club of San Buenaventura and did volunteer work for the county hospital and a home for unmarried mothers in Los Angeles.

All four daughters she had with Cash—Rosanne, Kathy, Cindy and Tara—graduated from St. Bonaventure High School in Ventura. Johnny had continued to support her

Rosanne Cash in performance in the mid-1990s. She remains a respected country artist in her own right today.

and their daughters financially through the years, and came back for their graduations.

Vivian Liberto died shortly after finishing her autobiography (*I Walked the Line: My Life with Johnny*). It had the tacit approval of Cash, with whom she had consulted before his death in the hope that he would allow his love letters to her to be published. He insisted on giving her approval in writing "because some publisher is sure to ask you for it."

She began her book by stating that "to me he is and will always be my wonderful, caring, protective husband,"

ending with the hope her daughters would now know more than ever "how much I loved their daddy."

The Cash children are still very active in preserving their father's music and legacy. Rosanne is a well respected-singer-songwriter in the country field, having charted twenty-one Top 40 country singles, eleven of which climbed to #1. She has received twelve Grammy nominations, winning in 1985. Cash also published four books and her essays and fiction have appeared in the *New York Times*, *Rolling Stone*, and *New York* magazine, among others. In 2014 released *The River & The Thread*, eleven original songs penned with

John Carter Cash and Kathy Cash accept an award for their father at the 37th Annual CMA Awards at the Grand Ole Opry House November 5, 2003, Nashville, Tennessee.

her long-time collaborator (and husband) John Leventhal, who also served as producer, arranger and guitarist.

Second oldest daughter Kathy Cash is married to bass player Jimmy Tittle. She met him when he was playing with Merle Haggard and she was a single parent, and over time he would be called upon to play with his father -in-law—notably on some of the American Recordings albums.

Cindy (Cynthia), who was married to Marty Stuart for five years from 1983, had performed with her father in the late 1980s when with a group called Next Generation which included Georgette Jones (daughter of Tammy Wynette and George Jones), Patsy Lynn (daughter of Loretta Lynn) and Cathy Twitty (daughter of Conway Twitty. After splitting with Stuart she married businessman Eddie Panetta, but he was killed in a motorcycle accident in 2009. This meant she lost four of the most significant people in her life, including June, Johnny and mother Vivian, in six short years.

Youngest daughter Tara Cash is a talented jewelry designer married to Milwaukee documentary filmmaker Fred Schwoebel, with two sons. In 2013 he premiered *The Mountains Will Wait for You*, a documentary on pioneering climber Grace Hudowalski. The forty-four-minute movie had lain in abeyance for many years while he was working on TV commercials, music videos and other projects, so his late father-in-law had completed the narration while still alive.

John Carter Cash is the self-appointed custodian of his father's musical legacy, curating his reissues. His mantra was "It has to be in line with what we believe my father would have wanted released."

When it came to unreleased material, Carter Cash maintained "the world would be a darker place" if the music was not released and it was "worth doing" if fans around the world wanted to hear it. "Do you want to see another Picasso if there's one that nobody has ever seen before?" he

Johnny Cash wrote two autobiographies, first *Man in Black: His Own Story in His Own Words* in 1975 and then *Cash: The Autobiography* (with Patrick Carr) in 1997. As might be expected, the publishing industry has produced many more books on the Man in Black—such as Steve Turner's authorized biography ("an honest look at an honest man"); Robert Hilburn (who was the chief music critic and pop music editor for the *Los Angeles Times*) wrote *Johnny Cash: The Life*. Covering the wider family are such titles as *Anchored in Love*, John Carter Cash's biography of his mother (above).

asked. "I would say that probably the world would want to see another Picasso… This is a work of art."

During the archiving of Cash's estate, it was revealed that his wife June Carter Cash had kept many master recording tapes. "They never threw anything away," said John Carter Cash. "They kept everything in their lives. They had an archive that had everything in it from the original audio tapes from *The Johnny Cash Show* to random things like a camel saddle, a gift from the prince of Saudi Arabia."

Although Cash was a singer-songwriter, few of his biggest hits are his own creations. Cash's songs have, however, been covered impressively by others, like Waylon Jennings' uptempo "Folsom Prison Blues," Ry Cooder's "Get Rhythm," and Nick Cave's "The Singer." He didn't find writing easy. "I start a lot more songs than I finish… Songwriting is a very strange thing as far as I'm concerned. It's not something that I can say, 'Next Tuesday morning, I'm gonna sit down and write songs.' "

As a songwriter, Cash had the ability to stir the soul. He kept his songs real. "It's like a novelist writing far out things. If it makes a point and makes sense, then people like to read that. But if it's off in left-field and goes over the edge, you lose it." To that end he not only wrote some memorable songs but also sourced many classics from other songwriters, giving them his own unique stamp. "When I record somebody else's song, I have to make it my own or it doesn't feel right. I'll say to myself, I wrote this and he doesn't know it!"

Communication and empathy with his audience was always Cash's watchword. "You've got a song you're singing from your gut, you want that audience to feel it in their gut. And you've got to make them think that you're one of them sitting out there with them too. They've got to be able to relate to what you're doing."

Of the Tennessee Three, Guitarist Luther Perkins, as

A wall of gold, silver and platinum discs at the Johnny Cash Museum.

already recounted, died in 1968 from injuries suffered in a house fire, while bassist Marshall Grant passed away, age eighty-three, in 2011.

Grant had played bass with Cash until 1980 when he began a career in management, handling The Statler Brothers until they retired in 2002 and later writing an autobiography titled *I Was There When It Happened*. Grant and Perkins were among the first inductees into the Musicians Hall of Fame in Nashville in 2007.

Drummer W.S. Holland had retired in 1997 after Cash quit touring, but reconsidered after the success of the movie *Walk The Line*. "It created a situation that people wanted to see somebody who was in the Johnny Cash band, so I'm still going," said the drummer, who continued to tour with the "Ultimate Johnny Cash Tribute Show" with Cash tribute artist Frank Hamilton & The New Tennessee Three. He also appeared on the History Channel show *Pawn Stars* on an episode titled "Cold Hard Cash" where he and a friend were selling a 1970 Rolls-Royce Johnny Cash once owned.

Though he registered many country chart-topping singles and albums, Johnny Cash had only released one album in his lifetime that reached the national #1 position—and that was a live recording of his San Quentin Prison show which hit the top in 1969.

He repeated the feat with a studio album two years after his death when *American V: A Hundred Highways*, his fifth collaboration with Rick Rubin, was released posthumously in 2006. Issued on Independence Day, the album debuted at #1 position on the *Billboard* Top 200 album chart for the week ending July 22.

And—not surprisingly, given the prolific nature of his final decade—that wasn't the last of the recordings in the vault. Three days before what would have been Cash's seventy-eighth birthday, in February 2010, *American VI: Ain't No Grave* made its appearance.

These unreleased recordings bolstered what was already a lucrative business for the Cash estate. In 2009, he sold more than three million records, reportedly earning more than $8m (£4.9m). But, prior to this sudden revenue upsurge, many of his belongings had been auctioned to pay estate taxes in excess of $10 million.

In September 2005, a three-day auction of Johnny and June's personal effects had taken place at Sotheby's in New York. The first day alone brought in in $1.24 million for items including a custom-made abalone-inlaid acoustic guitar that fetched $131,200.

Other items on offer in 769 separate lots included a photo of Elvis Presley signed to June ($18,000), a striped prisoner's jacket from Folsom Prison ($6,000), several black jackets, a 1987 Rolls Royce and the grand piano seen in the "Hurt" video.

The house on Caudill Drive in Hendersonville, the Cash family home for thirty-five years and the couple's main residence throughout their marriage, was placed on the market in June 2005 with an asking price of $2.9 million and included a 4.6-acre lakefront lot. Cash's younger brother, Tommy, the estate agent, said it would also include seven pieces of antique furniture, including the couple's

bed. Built in 1968, the house boasted seven bedrooms, five bathrooms and an outdoor swimming pool.

The house and grounds were bought by Bee Gee Barry Gibb for a reported $2.3 million. "This place will always be the spiritual home for the Cashes," Gibb said. "My wife, Linda, and I are determined to preserve it, to honor their memory. We fell in love with it. It's an incredible honor for us. We plan to use the home to write songs because of the musical inspiration."

Unfortunately, this was not to be as April 2007 saw the house destroyed in a fire during renovation work (see photos on pages 130–131). The House Of Cash museum, situated in

OPPOSITE: A 1997 Johnny Cash D-42 JC signature black Martin Guitar and a black duster coat are shown at a Sotheby's auction house press preview September 7, 2004.

BELOW: The handwritten lyrics of Johnny Cash's "When A Good Old Boy Goes Bad" are seen during the preview day of the "Icons and Idols" and property from the life and career of Johnny Cash auctions at Julien's Auctions in Beverly Hills, California on November 19, 2010.

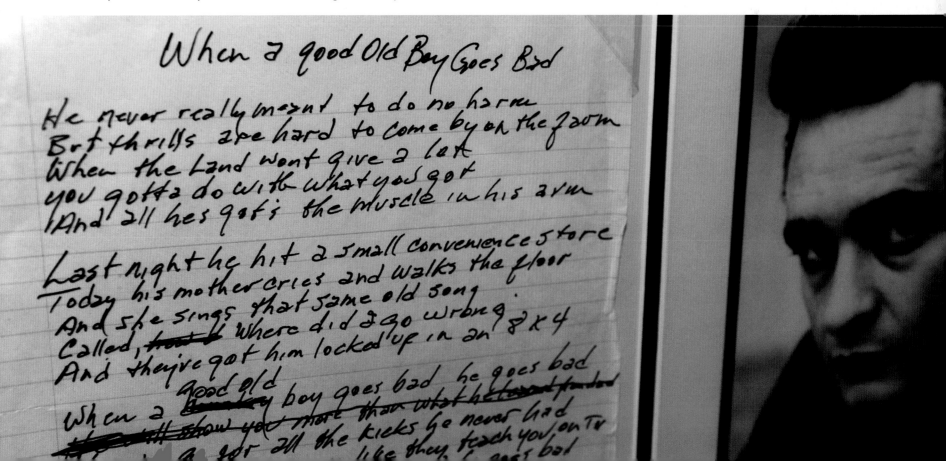

his former home, was lost in the fire. As had been apparent in footage used in the "Hurt" video, the museum had fallen into disrepair, the victim of a flood rather than neglect. Fortunately, there remained a main street in Hendersonville named Johnny Cash Parkway.

Steps are being taken to commemorate Johnny Cash by preserving items from his professional life. Unit One, Cash's tour bus from 1980 until 2003, was put on exhibit at the Rock and Roll Hall of Fame Museum in Cleveland, Ohio, in 2007. The prospect of a Johnny Cash Museum in Nashville excited a number of people—not least his daughter Kathy. "I'm excited about it; I think there should be something to honor dad in Nashville. There's not much. There's a mural downtown, and different artists honor him, but I think (the museum) is going to be really successful… I think it is important."

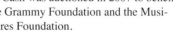

OPPOSITE: A Martin guitar signed by
Cash goes to auction in Beverly Hills, on
November 19, 2010.

ABOVE: Clothes and guitars owned by
Johnny and June came under the
hammer at Sotheby's in New York, 2004.

LEFT: This Alvarez Blue Guitar owned
by Cash was auctioned in 2007 to benefit
the Grammy Foundation and the Musi-
Cares Foundation.

Within five months of its grand opening in 2013, the latest attraction in Music City made it to the top of the Forbes "Must-See" Nashville destinations list. That prestigious acknowledgement was followed by *National Geographic* magazine putting it top of a list of worldwide "Pitch Perfect Museums" dedicated to a single musician. The Johnny Cash Museum beat the ABBA museum in Stockholm and the Kalakuta museum in Nigeria to first place. Exhibits include historical documents, letters, awards, costumes and instruments, interactive technology provided by the Nashville-based Griffin Technologies clamed to "take the visitor on a three-dimensional journey through Johnny Cash's life." The museum is based around the extensive and acclaimed collection of Bill Miller, a long-standing friend who founded the official Johnny Cash website.

This was augmented by items donated or lent by friends, colleagues and family members including his daughters, son and siblings. The collection features the earliest known Johnny Cash letters and documents as well as the handwritten manuscript to the last song he ever wrote. Visitors also are given an extensive look into Cash's offstage life including his childhood and his service in the United States Air Force.

Former vice president and friend Al Gore, one of the earliest visitors, and called it "A world-class collection of items that tells the story of Cash's life. I was blown away by how well it is put together. It's first class and you will see, you can mark my words, this will become one of the major tourist attractions for Nashville." Daughter Cindy Cash concurred: "Whatever anybody needs to know about my Dad that they don't know already is in that museum."

The awards and honors Cash picked up during his life continued to amass. One the family particularly appreciated was a limited-edition stamp that went on sale in June 2013. It featured a promotional picture of Cash taken around 1963. Daughter Tara remarked that: "Dad loved this country. I have no doubt that having his image on a United States postage stamp would be his proudest accomplishment. If Dad were here he'd be beaming with pride, and would say something to the effect of, 'Well. Ain't that somethin'? This face of mine on a postage stamp.' "

Johnny Cash was a man who used music to escape the drudgery and toil of his early life. But he never lost the common touch. When interviewed in 1987, he reflected that "For thirty-one years I've been staying in the finest hotels and traveling first class. But my roots are in the working man. I remember very well how it is to pick cotton ten hours a day, or to plough, or how to cut wood. I remember it so well, I guess, because I don't intend to ever try to do it again."

He never did.

OPPOSITE: The exterior of the Johnny Cash Museum pictured in 2013, its year of opening.

BELOW: The Johnny Cash stamp went on sale in 2013, commemorating the tenth anniversary of his death. Only 20 of 400,000 suggested subjects are selected for this honor.

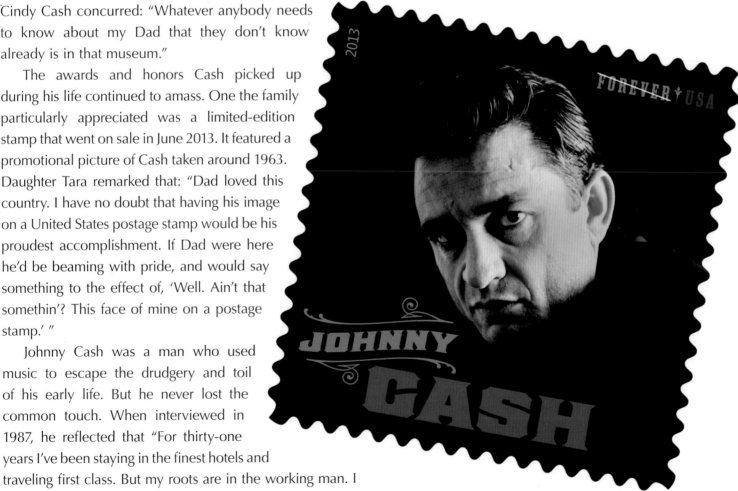

TOP TUNES: A SELECT DISCOGRAPHY OF HITS

SINGLES

1956

"I Walk the Line" #1 *Billboard* Hot Country Songs

"There You Go" #1 *Billboard* Hot Country Songs

1958

"Ballad of a Teenage Queen" #1 *Billboard* Hot Country Songs

"Guess Things Happen That Way" #1 *Billboard* Hot Country Songs

"The Ways of a Woman in Love" #2 *Billboard* Hot Country Songs

1959

"Don't Take Your Guns to Town" #1 *Billboard* Hot Country Songs

1963

"Ring of Fire" #1 *Billboard* Hot Country Songs

"The Matador" #2 *Billboard* Hot Country Songs

1964

"Understand Your Man" #1 *Billboard* Hot Country Songs

"The Ballad of Ira Hayes" #2 Canadian *RPM* Top Country

1965

"Orange Blossom Special" #2 Canadian *RPM* AC

1966

"The One on the Right Is on the Left" #2 *Billboard* Hot Country Songs

1967

"Rosanna's Going Wild" #2 *Billboard* Hot Country Songs, #1 Canadian *RPM* Top Country

"Jackson" (with June Carter Cash) #2 *Billboard* Hot Country Songs

1968

"Folsom Prison Blues" #1 *Billboard* Hot Country Songs, #1 Canadian *RPM* Top Country

"Daddy Sang Bass" #1 *Billboard* Hot Country Songs, #1 Canadian RPM Top Country

1969

"A Boy Named Sue" #1 *Billboard* Hot Country Songs/#2 AC/#1 Hot 100, #1 Canadian *RPM* Top Country

"Blistered" #1 Canadian RPM Top Country

"Get Rhythm" (re-release) #1 Canadian *RPM* Top Country

"If I Were a Carpenter" (with June Carter Cash) #2 *Billboard* Hot Country Songs, #1 Canadian *RPM* Top Country

1970

"What Is Truth" #1 Canadian RPM Top Country

"Sunday Mornin' Comin' Down" #1 *Billboard* Hot Country Songs, #1 Canadian *RPM* Top Country

"Flesh and Blood" #1 *Billboard* Hot Country Songs, #1 Canadian *RPM* Top Country

I WALK THE LINE
(CASH)
JOHNNY CASH

CORDS CORP., BOX 35, NARBERTH, PA 19072

MEMPHIS, TENNESSEE

1971

"Man in Black" #2 Canadian *RPM* Top Country

"A Thing Called Love" #2 *Billboard* Hot Country Songs,
   #1 Canadian *RPM* Top Country

1972

"Kate" #2 *Billboard* Hot Country Songs, #1 Canadian *RPM*
   Top Country

"Oney" #2 *Billboard* Hot Country Songs, #1 Canadian
   RPM Top Country

"Any Old Wind That Blows" #1 Canadian *RPM* Top Country

1976

"One Piece at a Time" #1 *Billboard* Hot Country Songs,
   #1 Canadian *RPM* Top Country/#1 *RPM* AC

1978

"There Ain't No Good Chain Gang" (with Waylon Jennings)
   #2 *Billboard* Hot Country Songs

1979

"(Ghost) Riders in the Sky" #2 *Billboard* Hot Country
   Songs, #1 Canadian *RPM* Top Country

ALBUMS

1963

Ring of Fire: The Best of Johnny Cash #1 *Billboard* Country
   (Gold)

1964

I Walk the Line #1 *Billboard* Country (US gold)

Bitter Tears: Ballads of the American Indian #2 *Billboard*
   Country

1967

Johnny Cash's Greatest Hits (compilation) #1 *Billboard*
   Country (US 2 x platinum; Can platinum)

1968

At Folsom Prison (live) #1 *Billboard* Country (US 3 x
   platinum; Can platinum)

1969

At San Quentin (live) #1 *Billboard* Country/#1 *Billboard*
   200/#1 Canadian *RPM* Top Country (US 3 x platinum;
   Can platinum)

Story Songs of the Trains and Rivers (compilation)
   #1 *Billboard* Country

1970

Hello, I'm Johnny Cash #1 *Billboard* Country

The World of Johnny Cash #2 *Billboard* Country

The Johnny Cash Show (live) #1 *Billboard* Country
   (US gold)

1971

Man in Black #1 *Billboard* Country

1972

A Thing Called Love #2 *Billboard* Country

1976

One Piece at a Time #2 *Billboard* Country

2005

The Legend of Johnny Cash (compilation) #2 *Billboard*
   Country (US 2 x platinum)

2006

American V: A Hundred Highways #1 *Billboard* Country/#1
   Billboard 200

2010

American VI: Ain't No Grave #2 *Billboard* Country

WHAT'S ON THE CD

1 "Cry! Cry! Cry!"
The B side of Cash's first single (A side "Mr Porter") "Cry! Cry! Cry!" was originally released on June 21, 1955, and was immediately successful, reaching #14 on the Country charts. Backed by the Tennessee Two—Luther Perkins on guitar and Marshall Grant on bass—it also appeared on his first LP, *With His Hot and Blue Guitar*, released in 1957.

2 "So Doggone Lonesome"
Recorded at Sun Records studios on July 30, 1955, Cash wrote the song with the Texas Troubadour, Ernest Dale Tubb in mind. Cash released the song on December 15, 1955, as B side to "Folsom Prison Blues." It reached #4 on the *Billboard* Country chart and appeared on his first album.

3 "Folsom Prison Blues"
One of Cash's signature songs which appeared on his debut album and also on *All Aboard the Blue Train*. Cash gained inspiration from the movie *Inside the Walls of Folsom Prison* (1951) which he saw in West Germany while a member of the USAF. Originally released on December 15, 1955, it was the re-release in April 1968 that reached #1 on both the *Billboard* (July 20–August 10) and *RPM* (July 20–August 3) country charts and the live performance of the song won Cash his first of four Grammy, the 1969 award for Best Country Vocal Performance, Male.

4 "I Walk the Line"
Written by Cash and recorded in 1956, "I Walk the Line" became his first *Billboard* #1, remaining there for six weeks and on the charts for over 43 weeks. Recorded on April 2 and released on May 1, it has sold over two million copies

with "Get Rhythm" as the B side. It also reached # 19 on the pop music charts.

5 "Get Rhythm"
Released in 1956 as the B-side to Cash's first #1, "I Walk the Line," in 1969, it was released as a single itself, with sound effects simulating a live recording. This rerelease went to #23 on the country charts and #1 on Canadian *RPM* Country Tracks between November 15 and November 22.

6 "Home of the Blues"
Written by Johnny Cash, Douglas L. McAlphin, and Glenn Douglas Tubb and produced by Jack Clement, "Home of the Blues" was recorded on July 1, 1957, and released as a single on August 10 with B side "Give My Love to Rose." The single reached #3 on the *Billboard* Hot Country Singles chart. It was also included on his second album *Sings the Songs That Made Him Famous*.

7 "Ballad of a Teenage Queen"
Written by Sun Records' Jack Clement it was recorded for the 1958 album *Sings the Songs That Made Him Famous*. Released as a single on January 6, 1958, it reached #1 on the *Billboard* Country charts and was a

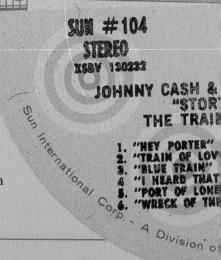

SUN #104
STEREO
ISBV 130232

JOHNNY CASH &
"STOR
THE TRAI

1. "HEY PORTER"
2. "TRAIN OF LOV
3. "BLUE TRAIN"
4. "I HEARD THAT
5. "PORT OF LONE
6. "WRECK OF THE

Sun International Corp. – A Division of

significant cross-over success reaching #14 on the *Billboard* Hot 100 making it one of his most successful early songs.

8 "Big River"
Released on the B-side of "Ballad of a Teenage Queen," "Big River" itself reached #4 on the *Billboard* country music charts. Originally recorded on October 11, 1957, with a verse omitted, it also appeared on the album *Sings the Songs That Made Him Famous*. The missing verse was aired in live performances and also appears—sung by Waylon Jennings—on the first Highwaymen album (1985).

9 "Guess Things Happen That Way"
This cross-over single was written by Jack Clement. and provided Cash's fourth #1 on the *Billboard* country chart. His eighth, released May 19, 1958, it spent eight weeks at #1 and twenty-four weeks on the chart. The B-side—"Come In Stranger"—reached #6.

10 "Don't Take Your Guns to Town"
Cash's fifth single to become a country #1, where it stayed for six weeks (February 23–March 30, 1959), "Don't Take Your Guns to Town" also reached #32 on the pop chart. It's also on the live album *VH1 Storytellers: Johnny Cash & Willie Nelson*.

11 "Little Drummer Boy"
Written by American classical music composer Katherine Kennicott Davis in 1941, Cash released a version of the song as a single in 1959—it reached #24 on the County charts

and #69 on the pop charts—and on his 1963 Christmas album, *The Christmas Spirit*.

12 "I Love You Because"
Another chart success, this 1949 song was written and recorded by Leon Payne. Johnny Cash's version was B-side to "Straight A's in Love" and it reached #20 in 1960.

13 "Oh Lonesome Me"
From the album *Now Here's Johnny Cash* was written and recorded in December 1957 by Don Gibson. The Cash version went to #13 in the country charts in 1961.

14 "Busted"
Written by Harlan Howard in 1962, "Busted" appeared on Cash's fifteenth album, *Blood, Sweat and Tears*. *Backed by the Carter Family*, the single reached #13 in the country charts.

15 "Ring of Fire"
Cowritten by June Carter Cash and Merle Kilgore, Cash's version of the song—originally recorded by June's sister, Anita Carter—first appeared on the 1963 album, *Ring of Fire: The Best of Johnny Cash*. Recorded on March 25, 1963, it was released on April 19 with "I'd Still Be There" as the B side and became the biggest hit of his career, staying at the top of the charts for seven weeks. It was certified Gold on January 21, 2010.

16 "Boy Named Sue"
Cash recorded Shel Silverstein's poem live at San Quentin State Prison at a concert on February 24, 1969. Filmed for TV and later released on the *At San Quentin* album, it became Cash's only top ten single on the *Billboard* Hot 100 where it spent three weeks at #2. It was #1 on the *Billboard* Hot Country Songs and Hot Adult Contemporary Tracks charts.

INDEX

A Gunfight, 98, 99, 100
ABC-TV, 60, 75, 126–135
Acuff, Roy, 15
Adams, Ryan, 141
Aggie Award, 126
Ahern, Brian, 108, 114
Albert Hall, 78
Almond, Marc, 124
American Recordings, 141, 146, 153, 156, 157, 166, 176
Anderson, Pink, 140
Anglin, Jack, 61
Armstrong, Louis, 75, 127
Arnold, Eddy, 132
Atkins, Chet, 68
Atkins, Ollie, 8
Atlanta State Prison, 88
Audioslave, 161
Autry, Gene, 58

Baez, Joan, 39
Ball, Earl Poole, 112
Ballard, Hank, 59
Baptist Hospital, 162
Barnhill, Jesse, 15
Bates, George, 19
Beatles, The, 77, 84
Beck, 152, 161
Bee Gees, 126, 181
Belafonte, Harry, 39
Betty Ford Clinic, 118
Billboard, 6, 27, 39, 46, 52, 54, 91, 94, 101, 132, 157, 180, 186, 187, 188, 189
Bisquera, Curt, 152
Black, Karen, 100, 101
Blake, Norman, 35, 68
Bland, Bobby Blue, 136
Bomba, David J., 172
Bono, 124, 141, 162, 169
Booker T and the MGs, 136
Bowen, Jimmy, 119
Bradley Film & Recording Studio, 38
Brock, Bill, 84, 85
Brooks & Dunn, 169

Brothers Four, The, 57,
Buckingham, Lindsey, 150, 152
Burnett, T-Bone, 173
Bush Laura, 157, 166
Bush, President George W., 157, 166
Byrds, The, 51

Cadillac, "One Piece At A Time," 8
Cale, J.J., 124
California, 40
Campbell, Glen, 103, 124, 140
Campbell, Mike, 152
Carnall, Stu, 40
Carnegie Hall, 57
Carr, Patrick, 176
Carson, Johnny, 40
Carter Cash, John, 74, 83, 95, 105, 107, 112, 114, 115, 117, 118, 124, 126, 136, 140, 161, 165, 175, 176, 178
Carter Cash, June, 9, 16, 51, 52, 59, 68, 69, 70, 71, 73, 77, 83, 88, 89, 90–93, 94, 98, 103, 104, 105, 106, 107, 110, 111, 112, 113, 114, 115, 124, 125, 126, 127, 130, 136, 138, 140, 141, 152, 155, 156, 161, 165, 166, 172, 174, 176, 178, 181, 189
Carter Family, 16, 51, 52, 55, 68, 69, 74, 90, 101, 108, 112, 136
Carter Sisters, 16, 17, 68
Carter, (Rebecca) Carlene, 68, 103, 112, 113, 115, 117, 127, 140, 141, 169
Carter, Alvin Pleasant "AP," 68
Carter, Anita, 52, 68, 152, 189
Carter, Helen, 68, 152
Carter, Maybelle, 16, 17, 68, 69, 110, 111, 125, 152, 158
Carter, Sara, 68
Cash Country, 140, 141
Cash, (Cynthia) Cindy, 27, 42, 59, 68, 116, 154, 174, 176, 185

Cash, (Kathleen) Kathy, 27, 40, 42, 75, 173, 174, 175, 176, 182
Cash, Carrie Rivers, 10, 13, 15, 16, 22, 42, 43, 73, 124, 136
Cash, Jack, 15, 74
Cash, Joann, 15
Cash, Ray, 10, 13, 15, 17, 42, 66, 90
Cash, Reba, 15
Cash, Reuben, 10
Cash, Rosanne, 21, 27, 42, 58, 88, 103, 112, 126, 140, 141, 166, 173, 174, 175
Cash, Roy, 15, 19
Cash, Tara, 42, 174, 176, 185
Cash, Tommy, 15, 58, 131, 181
Cash, William, 10
Cave, Nick, 166, 178
CBS/Columbia, 32, 98, 127, 149
Central Park Summer-Stage, 145
Chapin, Harry, 124
Charles, Ray, 71, 75, 127
Cherry, Hugh, 84
Chuck Wagon Gang, 38
Clapton, Eric, 75
Clark, Roy, 134
Clayton, Adam, 124
Clement, Jack, 35, 36, 52, 112, 115, 121, 124, 136, 188, 189
Clooney, Rosemary, 19
Cohen, Leonard, 147, 149
Columbia Records, 37, 38, 39, 40, 46, 85, 101, 114, 115, 119, 121
Columbo, 98
Cooder, Ry, 178
Cooke, Sam, 156
Corbijn, Anton, 9, 147
Cornell, Chris, 152
Costello, Elvis, 124, 127
Country Music Hall of Fame, 6, 40, 48, 113, 116-117, 126, 150, 165
Country Music Holiday, 68
Cousin Jody, 103
Cramer, Floyd, 46, 48

Creedence Clearwater Revival, 127
Crow, Sheryl, 166, 167, 168
Crowell, Rodney, 112, 126, 166, 169
Cumberland Heights, 136
Cummins Prison, 82, 86

Dalhart, Vernon, 16
Danzig, Glen, 147
David, Hal, 152
Davis, Clive, 50
Davis, Jimmie, 35
Davis, Katherine Kennicott, 189
Davis, Oscar, 103
Def American, 141, 146
Dehr, Richard, 152
Depp, Johnny, 146
Derek and the Dominos, 127
Dew, Holly, 46
Dextel, Al, 38
Diamond, Neil, 157
Dixie Rhythm Ramblers, 19
Door-to-Door Maniac, 64
Douglas, Kirk, 98, 101
Dr Quinn Medicine Woman, 98
Drake, Guy, 94
Duvall, Robert, 139
Dyess, AK., 10, 11, 12–13, 15, 17, 68
Dylan, Bob, 39, 51, 54, 55, 57, 59, 71, 75, 88, 94, 115, 129, 136, 140, 141, 144, 154, 172

Eagles, The, 157
Eavis, Michael, 148, 150
Edmunds, Dave, 113
El Paso, 66
Encino, 40
Ensign, Dennis, 66
Epstein, Howie, 117, 152
Eshleman, Paul, 109
Evangel Temple Choir, 101
Evans, Marilyn, 37
Explo 72, 109, 110, 111